Young Person's Guide to Getting and Keeping a Good Job

Third Edition

The JIST course used successfully by more than 100,000 students!

Michael Farr
Marie A. Pavlicko, Ed.D.

JIST Works
America's Career Publisher

Young Person's Guide to Getting and Keeping a Good Job, Third Edition

Except for the material in Chapter 8 that appears in *Creating Your High School Resume: A Step-by-Step Guide to Preparing an Effective Resume for College and Career* (JIST Publishing, Inc) by Kathryn Kraemer Troutman. All rights reserved. Used with permission.

Published by JIST Works, an imprint of JIST Publishing, Inc.
8902 Otis Avenue
Indianapolis, IN 46216-1033

Phone: 1-800-648-JIST   Fax: 1-800-JIST-FAX
E-mail: info@jist.com   Web site: www.jist.com

Note to Instructors: This workbook was written to support a course on career planning, job search methods, and job survival skills for high school juniors and seniors. The course can be presented as a minicurriculum within other courses or as a separate course.

An instructor's guide (ISBN 1-59357-086-4) is available separately to support this workbook and is essential for its presentation in class or group settings. It will save you many hours of session planning. This comprehensive guide contains activities to support each chapter, including discussion topics, assignments, and more. A separate CD-ROM of instructor's resources (ISBN 1-59357-088-0) reinforces all major topics covered in the student workbook. It includes PowerPoint slides that are excellent for seminars, workshops, and large classes. Also available separately is the *Data Minder* (ISBN 1-59357-087-2) in packages of 10. A single copy is attached to the inside back cover of this book. JIST also offers the *Job Search Knowledge Scale* (ISBN 1-59357-105-4) and numerous videos and DVDs as tools to reinforce the concepts in this workbook.

Quantity discounts are available for JIST books. Have future editions of JIST books automatically delivered to you on publication through our convenient standing order program. Call 1-800-648-JIST for a free catalog and more information.

Visit our Web site at **www.jist.com** for information on JIST, free job search tips, book excerpts, and ways to order our many products. For free information on 14,000 job titles, visit **www.careeroink.com**.

Development Editors: Heather Stith, Barb Terry
Cover and Interior Designer: Aleata Howard
Production Editor: Karen A. Gill
Interior Layout: Toi Davis, Aleata Howard
Proofreader: Jeanne Clark

The publisher acknowledges the contributions of Gayle O. MacDonald, M.Ed., to the previous editions of this book. The publisher thanks Laura Giese, Mundelein High School, Mundelein, Illinois, for reviewing the *Young Person's Guide to Getting and Keeping a Good Job* products.

Printed in Canada

11 10 09 08 07 06   9 8 7 6 5 4 3 2 1

ISBN-10 1-59357-085-6

ISBN-13 978-1-59357-085-9

About This Book

This workbook will show you how to find a good job—even if you don't have paid work experience yet. What is a good job? Most people would agree that one element of a good job is that it suits your skills and interests.

Although this book assumes that you have some idea about what you want to do, the material will be helpful even if you don't know or are looking for part-time or summer work or an internship. Even if you don't plan to look for a job soon, the material is important because it encourages you to think about what you want out of life and what you have to offer.

The content of this easy-to-use book is based on extensive research on the most effective job search methods and job survival skills available. The first edition of this book was tested with thousands of students before it was published, and many more thousands have used it and the second edition since. Those students, in addition to their teachers, have helped us improve this edition.

Through clear explanations, worksheets, and examples, this book will help you to:

- ✔ Understand an employer's expectations
- ✔ Discover and present your skills
- ✔ Document your work and school experiences
- ✔ Learn effective job search techniques
- ✔ Write good applications, cover letters, and resumes
- ✔ Find references who can talk about your skills

- ✔ Handle yourself well in interviews
- ✔ Answer even the toughest interview questions
- ✔ Create a career portfolio
- ✔ Organize your schedule to get a good job in less time
- ✔ Get ahead on a new job
- ✔ Explore career options
- ✔ Consider starting your own business

The small *Data Minder* attached to the inside back cover of this workbook lets you record the details needed during your job search. Fill it in, carry it with you, and use it as you complete applications, write your resume, and go on interviews.

We hope this workbook helps you learn some good things about yourself—and helps you get off to a good start in your career and your life. We wish you well.

Contents

Preface

You are fortunate to attend a program that teaches you the material in this workbook. Most people are not so fortunate. The authors, for example, did not learn anything about job seeking in high school or college. They did not take a career test. In short, no one helped us with our career or job search planning. We turned out well, but we would have had a much easier time if we had been offered this type of training.

This book is easy to use, but you should know that the content is based on extensive research on the most effective job search methods and job survival skills available. Millions of people have used the JIST job search techniques to find better jobs in less time. The techniques we recommend *do* work. But they will work only if you are willing to use them. If you plan to get a full-time, part-time, or summer job in the next few months or years, this workbook will help. We wrote it to give you the basics you need to obtain a new job and to do it well.

Even if you don't plan to look for a job soon, this material is important for other reasons. It will encourage you to think about what you want out of life and what you have to offer. Can you, for example, list your skills? Can you tell someone what you do well? You will learn to answer these questions—and many more.

Thousands of students tested the first edition of this workbook before it was published, and many more thousands have used it since. Those students and their teachers have helped us improve this edition. Thanks for your enthusiasm! The editors and designers at JIST have also helped greatly in making this book look and "work" better.

The third edition contains many new and improved features, including the following:

- ✔ Additional information on using the Internet in your job search
- ✔ The latest in technology—from electronic resumes and planners to digital portfolios and online applications
- ✔ Updated statistics and career information
- ✔ Coverage of SCANS skills that are so important to employers
- ✔ More information on entrepreneurships because many people are choosing to own their own businesses rather than be employed by others
- ✔ References to service-learning, an excellent way to meet new people and build stronger networks
- ✔ A new design with revised and reorganized pages for easy reading and use

Let's get started!

Chapter 1

An Introduction to Finding a Good Job

You probably already know some things about finding a job. Perhaps you have found part-time jobs in the past. Your job now is to learn how to find a good job and how to find it in less time.

Before looking for a job, you must know how to identify the skills you have and learn some new ones. You should have some idea of what type of job you are qualified for. Finally, you must learn how to improve the job search techniques you already know.

Job-Seeking Skills Can Improve Your Career and Your Life

During the years you work, you will probably change jobs and even careers many times. Knowing how to find a good job is a valuable skill that can make a difference in your career and your life.

Many adult job seekers have never learned effective job-seeking skills. In fact, most have never read a book on how to find a job. As a result, they often are unemployed far longer than they need to be. And they often take jobs that don't give them the pay and satisfaction another job might.

Job-seeking skills can help you obtain more rewarding jobs throughout your life.

66*Character cannot be developed in ease and quiet. Only through experience of trial and suffering can the soul be strengthened, ambition inspired, and success achieved.*99

Helen Keller

ACTIVITY

The Job Search Quiz

This quiz is designed to help you discover what you know about looking for work. It will also help you think about your job search. Your answers will not be graded. Read each question carefully and answer it as well as you can.

1. Name five reasons why people stay unemployed.

   _____

   _____

   _____

   _____

   _____

2. What are the top three reasons that employers give for screening out (not hiring) job seekers? _____

   _____

   _____

   _____

3. List five of your best or most important skills. (Note: These skills don't have to be job related. They should be things you do particularly well.)

   _____

   _____

   _____

   _____

   _____

4. What are the two most effective techniques for finding a job?_____

_____

_____

_____

5. How many hours per week should you invest in a job search?_____

6. What percentage of all jobs is advertised?_____

7. What is the real purpose of an application form?_____

_____

_____

_____

8. What size organizations hire the most people?_____

9. How many weeks is the average job seeker unemployed?_____

10. How often does the average person change jobs?_____

11. How often will the average worker change careers in his lifetime?

_____

12. What is the unemployment rate in your region? _____

You will learn the answers to these and other questions in this course. Some answers may surprise you. You will learn that the more you know about yourself and the job market, the more likely you will find a good job.

Getting a Job *Is* a Job

Getting a job is a job in itself. The harder you work at it, the better your chances are of getting the job you want.

> Like other things you have learned, this course will require some effort. But the advantages to you are great. Whether you are presently working, looking for work, planning to enter the job market after graduation, or planning to further your education beyond high school, you need to know the basics of how to find a job.

Millions of people have used the JIST job search techniques to find better jobs in less time. The techniques in this book *do* work. But they will work only if you are willing to use them.

Chapter 2

An Employer's Expectations

Sometimes, the best way to know what employers expect of you is to find out what they look for in other job seekers. This chapter will teach you to think like an employer and examine just what employers look for in the people they hire.

The important question you need to answer is "Do I meet an employer's expectations?"

ACTIVITY

What Does an Employer Expect?

In this activity, you will work with a small group of other students to role-play operating your own company. You are to complete the following tasks:

1. Appoint a group member to be a company recorder. The recorder will write down all the ideas that your group comes up with on the following worksheet.

2. Give your group a company name and list its type of product or service.

3. Make up a list of the types of positions that your company needs to employ.

4. Write down the characteristics that you think are important to look for in potential employees. Make your list as long as possible. Try to name 15 to 20 things. Your list can also include characteristics that would prevent your company from hiring certain applicants.

EMPLOYEE CHARACTERISTICS WORKSHEET

Company name: _____

Product or service: _____

_____

Types of positions that your company wants to fill: _____

_____

_____

_____

_____

_____

_____

List the most important characteristics to look for in potential employees. Don't worry whether the ideas seem good or bad. Just list every idea that your group has.

_____

_____

_____

_____

_____

_____

_____

_____

_____

List key ideas from other groups:

_____

_____

_____

_____

_____

_____

_____

_____

ACTIVITY

The Three Major Employer Expectations

Employers know what they expect from people who apply for jobs. The important question you need to answer is, "Do I meet an employer's expectations?"

Before you answer this, take a closer look at yourself and review the major points that an employer looks for in an interview. The following worksheets on each expectation will help you prepare for job interviews. After each one, you get your turn to list the ways that you can improve or show an employer that you meet the expectations for the job.

EMPLOYER'S EXPECTATION 1— PERSONAL APPEARANCE

Do you look like the right person for the job?

1. How would you dress for an interview?_____

_____

_____

2. Who in the room looks like the best person for a job, based on the way he or she appears right now (clothes, grooming, manner of talking, and so on)?

_____

3. What special qualities about that person stand out and make him or her look like the best fit for a job?_____

_____

_____

4. What would you do to make a good first impression?_____

_____

_____

Would your manner make the interviewer want to hire you?

1. How does the way you normally act compare with the way you would act during an interview?_____

_____

_____

2. What can you do to avoid becoming nervous in an interview?_____

_____

_____

3. Is it better to be quiet and shy in an interview or more assertive—and possibly be seen as pushy? Why?_____

_____

_____

4. What interview behaviors might an employer react to in a negative way?

_____

_____

How else can you make an impression? How could each of the following impress an employer?

1. Your paper tools (application, resume, portfolio, and so on):_____

_____

_____

2. Phone conversations with the employer:_____

_____

_____

(continued)

(continued)

3. What others say about you: _____

_____

_____

_____

TIP First impressions count! Did you know that of all job seekers, about 40 percent get rejected because of poor personal appearance? If you do not make a positive first impression with an employer, you probably won't get hired.

YOUR TURN

Meeting Expectation 1

Think about the way you dress and speak and what your body language and behavior say about you. Also consider the way your resume and application look and how good your references are. You want to show the employer that you are professional, confident, and capable. Now write three things that you could improve to meet an employer's expectation of personal appearance.

1. _____

_____

2. _____

_____

3. _____

_____

ACTIVITY

EMPLOYER'S EXPECTATION 2—ATTENDANCE, PUNCTUALITY, AND DEPENDABILITY

Can you be counted on to do the job?

1. Why would an employer be interested in your attendance record?

   _____

   _____

2. When is the best time to arrive for an interview? Why?_____

   _____

   _____

3. What does the expression "Time is money" mean to you?_____

   _____

   _____

4. Have you been reliable in the past, either in school or on a previous job? Give examples:_____

   _____

   _____

5. Why is an employer interested in how long you might stay on the job?

   _____

   _____

Employers will not hire you unless they are sure you are dependable and can get the job done. Someone who is unreliable or who will leave too soon after learning the job is not worth the trouble of hiring and training. Many employers will hire a person with fewer credentials over a more experienced person if they believe that the less experienced person will be more reliable.

YOUR TURN

Meeting Expectation 2

Give examples of how you would show an employer that you have the following characteristics:

1. Good attendance record: _____

   _____

2. Punctuality: _____

   _____

3. Reliability: _____

   _____

If you make a good first impression and convince the employer that you can be counted on (employer expectations 1 and 2), then your ability to do the job becomes important. The following worksheet gives some points to consider.

"*Knowledge is power.*"
Francis Bacon

ACTIVITY

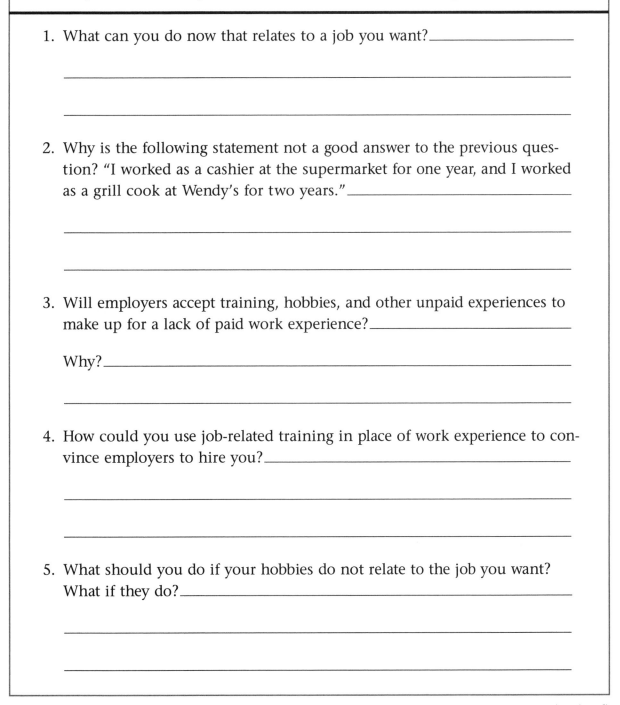

EMPLOYER'S EXPECTATION 3—
SKILLS, EXPERIENCE, AND TRAINING

1. What can you do now that relates to a job you want?_____
   _____
   _____

2. Why is the following statement not a good answer to the previous question? "I worked as a cashier at the supermarket for one year, and I worked as a grill cook at Wendy's for two years."_____
   _____
   _____

3. Will employers accept training, hobbies, and other unpaid experiences to make up for a lack of paid work experience?_____
   Why?_____
   _____

4. How could you use job-related training in place of work experience to convince employers to hire you?_____
   _____
   _____

5. What should you do if your hobbies do not relate to the job you want? What if they do?_____
   _____
   _____

(continued)

(continued)

6. What would volunteer work tell an employer about you?_____

_____

_____

7. Why is it important to translate life experiences into informal training and state them in years (or months)?_____

_____

TIP

Job-related skills are important to an employer. Most employers will consider your training and other life experience to make up for shortcomings in work experience. Many employers will hire someone who they are convinced will be reliable and hard working. Employers can often train this kind of person on the job to make up for a lack of experience.

YOUR TURN

Meeting Expectation 3

Write three things that you could say to an employer in an interview to help meet an employer's expectation of job skills:

1. _____

_____

2. _____

_____

3. _____

_____

ACTIVITY

Survey of Employers

This activity will give you an opportunity to learn what local employers look for. You are to visit or call at least one employer before the next class. The employer can be someone you already know—like an uncle, for example. You can also look up an employer in the yellow pages of the phone book or simply drop in on an employer on your way home from school. As you make your call or visit, use the following survey form to record your information. Here are some steps and important reminders:

1. Get to the person in charge and list the name, job title, and contact information of that person.

2. Ask the three survey questions that are listed on the worksheet that follows.

3. Record the employer's responses on the survey sheet.

4. Be ready to report your findings to the class at the next session.

Employers are people, so they will react in different ways to your asking them questions. But most students who do this activity find the following to be true:

✔ Most employers are friendly. They are willing to answer your questions.

✔ Although employers may use different words to explain what they want in employees, it usually fits into one of the three employer expectations.

✔ The employers "dropped in on" might be willing to hire you or your class-mates in the future!

EMPLOYER'S EXPECTATIONS
TELEPHONE/ON-SITE SURVEY WORKSHEET

Organization name:_____

Address:_____

Employer's name:_____

Employer's job title:_____

(continued)

(continued)

Phone number:_____ E-mail address:_____

What you should do

1. Introduce yourself by saying, *Hello, my name is*_____.

   *I am a student at*_____.

2. Ask to talk to the person in charge, and find out his or her name. *May I please talk to the person in charge, or may I speak with Mr. (or Mrs. or Ms.)*_____?

3. When you speak to that person, introduce yourself again. Explain that you are doing an assignment for school and would like to ask a few questions about what he or she looks for in a good worker.

4. Ask the following three questions, and record the answers in the spaces given.

   *Could you please tell me what you look for in a person you hire?*_____

   _____

   _____

   _____

   What are the top three skills needed by the people who work here?

   _____

   _____

   *What are the most important personality traits for people who do this type of work?*_____

   _____

   _____

5. Thank the employer for the time he or she spent with you.

Chapter 3

Identify Your Skills

Employers want to know what skills you will bring to the job. You must be able to identify and give examples of your skills in an interview. Of all job seekers, 80 to 85 percent cannot describe their job skills in an interview. Knowing what you can do well is an important part of your job search and your life.

YOUR TURN

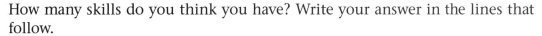

What Are Your Skills?

How many skills do you think you have? Write your answer in the lines that follow.

1. _____

2. _____

3. _____

4. _____

5. _____

6. _____

7. _____

8. _____

9. _____

10. _____

Three Types of Skills

Each person has hundreds of skills. To better understand them, think of your set of skills as a triangle, with each side representing a different category of skills.

Following are brief definitions of each type of skill. The activities that follow will help you identify your self-management, transferable, and job-related skills.

Self-Management

Job-Related

Transferable

✔ **Self-management skills:** These skills help you adapt and do well in new situations. They include your personality, your ability to get along with others, and your ability to fit into the work situation. Some examples of using these skills include being reliable, cooperating with others, and being willing to work hard.

✔ **Transferable skills:** These are the skills you can use in many different jobs. An auto mechanic, for example, needs to be good with his hands, and an administrative assistant must be well organized. These skills can also be used in or transferred to many other types of jobs. For example, a carpenter also must be good with his hands, and a librarian must be well organized.

✔ **Job-related skills:** These skills are needed in a particular job. An auto mechanic, for example, must be familiar with tools and repair procedures, and an accountant must know balance sheets and computerized accounting systems.

The system of dividing skills into three categories is not perfect. And some things, such as being trustworthy, dependable, and well organized, are considered both personality traits and skills.

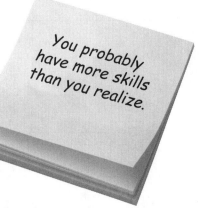

You probably have more skills than you realize.

Some overlap exists between the three skills categories. For example, a skill such as being organized can be considered either a self-management or a transferable skill. For our purposes, however, the skills categories are a useful system for identifying skills that are important in the job search.

When you list your skills, be as honest and accurate about yourself as possible. Make sure that you can back up each of your skills with an example.

SCANS Skills

In the early 1990s, the U.S. Secretary of Labor appointed a commission to study what skills young people need to succeed in the workplace. The skills that this commission found to be most important are known as SCANS (Secretary's Commission on Achieving Necessary Skills) skills. These skills are divided into two main groups: foundation skills and workplace competencies.

Foundation skills include skills from the self-management and transferable categories. You need to have these skills before you can develop workplace competencies. There are three main kinds of foundation skills:

✔ **Basic skills:** Reading, writing, mathematics, speaking, and listening skills are essential for workplace success.

✔ **Thinking skills:** Being able to learn, make decisions, and solve problems are examples of thinking skills.

✔ **Personal qualities:** Employers want employees who show individual responsibility, self-esteem, self-control, the ability to get along with others, and honesty.

Workplace competencies include skills from the transferable and job-related categories. These competencies are divided into five groups:

✔ **Resources:** This group involves managing time, money, materials, and people. Examples of these skills are budgeting, scheduling, and supervising.

✔ **Interpersonal skills:** This group involves working with people. Examples of these skills are teaching, serving customers, and working with a team.

✔ **Technology:** This group involves working with tools and machines. Examples of these skills are maintaining, repairing, and troubleshooting.

✔ **Systems:** This group involves working with processes. Examples of these skills include creating charts and diagrams, monitoring and improving systems, and designing.

✔ **Information:** This group involves working with data. Examples of these skills include using computers, researching, and organizing information.

Schools focus on developing students' SCANS skills through classwork. As you list your skills in the following activities, think about work you have done both in and outside of school that has prepared you for a good job.

ACTIVITY

Identify Your Self-Management Skills

This activity will help you identify your self-management skills. Remember to be honest with yourself.

GOOD-WORKER TRAITS

List three things about yourself that, in your opinion, make you a good worker.

1. _____

2. _____

3. _____

SELF-MANAGEMENT SKILLS CHECKLIST

Check all the skills that apply to you. Be sure you can prove your skills with specific examples.

Key Skills

All employers highly value the following skills. They often won't hire a person who does not have most or all of these skills:

- ☐ Able to coordinate
- ☐ Technology/computer savvy
- ☐ Dependable
- ☐ Able to follow instructions
- ☐ Get along with coworkers
- ☐ Get along with supervisor

- ☐ Have good attendance
- ☐ Have positive attitude
- ☐ Hard working
- ☐ Honest
- ☐ Able to meet deadlines
- ☐ Punctual

Other Self-Management Skills

- ☐ Adaptive
- ☐ Adventurous
- ☐ Ambitious
- ☐ Assertive

- ☐ Capable
- ☐ Careful
- ☐ Cheerful
- ☐ Competent

- ☐ Cooperative
- ☐ Creative
- ☐ Dedicated
- ☐ Efficient
- ☐ Energetic
- ☐ Enthusiastic
- ☐ Flexible
- ☐ Formal
- ☐ Friendly
- ☐ Good attitude
- ☐ Good-natured
- ☐ Helpful
- ☐ Highly motivated
- ☐ Humble

- ☐ Imaginative
- ☐ Independent
- ☐ Industrious
- ☐ Inquisitive
- ☐ Intelligent
- ☐ Loyal
- ☐ Mature
- ☐ Methodical
- ☐ Motivated
- ☐ Open-minded
- ☐ Optimistic
- ☐ Original
- ☐ Patient
- ☐ Persistent

- ☐ Physically strong
- ☐ Polite
- ☐ Quick learner
- ☐ Reliable
- ☐ Resourceful
- ☐ Self-confident
- ☐ Self-motivated
- ☐ Sense of humor
- ☐ Sincere
- ☐ Solve problems
- ☐ Steady
- ☐ Tactful
- ☐ Take pride in work
- ☐ Trustworthy

Additional Self-Management Skills

Add any self-management skills you have that are not on the list.

_____

_____

_____

YOUR TURN

Your Top Five Self-Management Skills

Now go back through the lists of good-worker traits and self-management skills. Circle the five you feel are most important for an employer to know about you.

For each of these five skills, give a good example of when you used that skill. The examples can be from work, school, family experiences, or another type of life experience.

1. Skill:_____

   Example:_____

   _____

(continued)

(continued)

_____

_____

2. Skill: _____

   Example: _____

   _____

   _____

   _____

3. Skill: _____

   Example: _____

   _____

   _____

   _____

4. Skill: _____

   Example: _____

   _____

   _____

   _____

5. Skill: _____

   Example: _____

   _____

   _____

   _____

ACTIVITY

Identify Your Transferable Skills

As in the previous activity, check all the skills in the checklist that apply to you. Be sure that you can prove them with specific examples.

TRANSFERABLE SKILLS CHECKLIST

Key Skills

These skills tend to get you higher levels of responsibility and pay. For this reason, they are worth emphasizing in interviews.

- ☐ Accept criticism
- ☐ Accept responsibility
- ☐ Communicate in writing with others
- ☐ Complete assignments
- ☐ Cooperate with others/team player
- ☐ Increase sales or efficiency
- ☐ Instruct others
- ☐ Manage money or budgets
- ☐ Meet deadlines

- ☐ Meet the public
- ☐ Negotiate
- ☐ Organize or manage projects
- ☐ Solve problems
- ☐ Speak in public
- ☐ Supervise others
- ☐ Take pride in doing a good job
- ☐ Understand budgets
- ☐ Be willing to learn

Other Transferable Skills
Using my hands/dealing with things

- ☐ Assemble or make things
- ☐ Build, observe, or inspect things
- ☐ Construct or repair buildings
- ☐ Drive or operate vehicles
- ☐ Follow safety procedures

- ☐ Work well with hands
- ☐ Install/test
- ☐ Make new things
- ☐ Observe/inspect
- ☐ Operate tools and machinery

Dealing with data

- ☐ Analyze data or facts
- ☐ Audit records
- ☐ Budget
- ☐ Calculate or compute numbers
- ☐ Check for accuracy/proofread
- ☐ Compare, inspect, or record facts
- ☐ Compare/compile data
- ☐ Evaluate data

- ☐ Keep financial records
- ☐ Locate answers or information
- ☐ Manage money
- ☐ Observe/inspect
- ☐ Pay attention to details
- ☐ Record facts
- ☐ Research or investigate data
- ☐ Take inventory

Working with people

- ☐ Care for patients
- ☐ Comfort others
- ☐ Counsel people
- ☐ Demonstrate
- ☐ Be diplomatic/tactful
- ☐ Display leadership skills
- ☐ Help others
- ☐ Offer insights
- ☐ Instruct/teach others
- ☐ Interview people
- ☐ Act kind
- ☐ Listen carefully
- ☐ Negotiate
- ☐ Be outgoing
- ☐ Be patient
- ☐ Persuade others
- ☐ Act pleasant
- ☐ Respect others
- ☐ Be sociable
- ☐ Be tactful
- ☐ Tolerate others
- ☐ Understand/trust others

Using words and ideas

- ☐ Articulate/speak clearly
- ☐ Ask questions/inquire
- ☐ Communicate verbally
- ☐ Correspond with others
- ☐ Create new ideas
- ☐ Edit
- ☐ Follow directions
- ☐ Invent
- ☐ Be logical
- ☐ Remember information
- ☐ Research
- ☐ Speak in public
- ☐ Use correct reasoning/logic
- ☐ Write clearly

Leadership

- ☐ Arrange social functions
- ☐ Compete against others
- ☐ Act decisive
- ☐ Delegate duties
- ☐ Direct others
- ☐ Explain things to others
- ☐ Get results
- ☐ Make decisions
- ☐ Mediate problems
- ☐ Motivate people
- ☐ Negotiate agreements
- ☐ Plan activities
- ☐ Run meetings
- ☐ Be self-controlled
- ☐ Solve problems
- ☐ Supervise or manage others
- ☐ Take risks

Dealing with technology

- ☐ Code, enter, and debug programs
- ☐ Design Web pages
- ☐ Enter data
- ☐ Install/troubleshoot programs
- ☐ Operate computer systems
- ☐ Perform basic accounting tasks
- ☐ Perform desktop publishing functions
- ☐ Perform word processing functions
- ☐ Use the Internet
- ☐ Use various software programs

Additional Transferable Skills

Add any transferable skills you have that are not on the list.

_____

_____

YOUR TURN
Your Top Five Transferable Skills

Now go back through the list of transferable skills. Circle the top five that you want to use in your next job. For each of these five skills, give a good example of when you used that skill.

1. Skill:_____

    Example:_____

    _____

2. Skill:_____

    Example:_____

    _____

3. Skill:_____

    Example:_____

    _____

4. Skill:_____

    Example:_____

    _____

5. Skill:_____

    Example:_____

    _____

ACTIVITY

Identify Your Job-Related Skills

Each job requires skills related to that particular job. You can learn some job-related skills quickly, whereas others may take years of training. These skills are in addition to the self-management and transferable skills you need to succeed in that job.

JOB-RELATED SKILLS WORKSHEET

Even if you have not yet worked in the job you want, you probably have some experience that relates to it. This experience usually comes from several sources: courses you have taken; other jobs or volunteer work; and hobbies, family activities, and other experiences. In Chapter 4, you will detail all of your experience, but this activity will give you practice matching the job-related skills you have to a specific position.

You should have some idea of the type of job you want and the skills that the job requires. Even if you are not sure, write the title of a job that interests you here. (Check the listing of job titles in the appendix for help if you need it.)

1. List classes or vocational training you have taken or school projects you have completed that relate to this job. Include certificates you have earned that are necessary for this job:_____

    _____

    _____

2. Think about the skills you have used in other work or volunteer experiences, and then list the skills that would apply to the job you chose. For example, list specific computer programs, machines, or tools that you know how to use. Also list specific responsibilities you have had in previous jobs.

    _____

    _____

---

3. List skills you have gained in hobbies, family activities, extracurricular activities, and other experiences outside of work or school that relate to this job. For example, if you want to work as a bookkeeper, you would list the fact that when you were student council treasurer, you had to maintain financial records and make bank deposits.

_____

_____

_____

"If you have built castles in the air, your work need not be lost; that is where they should be. Now put the foundations under them."

Henry David Thoreau

Chapter 4

Document Your Education, Experience, and References

Telling an employer you can do a job is not enough. You have to prove it. You can do this by showing concrete examples of your experience and knowledge. These examples can come from many different areas, including school, paid and unpaid work, hobbies, and everyday life. You also need references who can confirm your abilities and strengths.

Organize Your School and Work Background

The following activities will help you collect and organize information about your educational background, school experiences, training, honors, and hobbies. In addition, you will list your work experiences, including paid and unpaid jobs and volunteer work. In each activity, think about the points that an employer might want to know about you. An example is your skills.

Remember that all jobs and experiences are valuable, no matter how little they pay or how small they seem. Employers are interested in what you can do. All experiences can help prove that you are a good worker.

“There is no knowledge, no light, no wisdom that you are in possession of, but what you have received it from some source.”

Brigham Young

Introducing the *Data Minder* Booklet

The activities that follow match the small, portable *Data Minder* booklet attached in the back of this workbook. You can use the *Data Minder* as your personal job search assistant. It is designed to help you remember the many details that you will need throughout your job search, such as dates, phone numbers, addresses, and information about your background.

You can carry the *Data Minder* with you after you complete it. Your *Data Minder* will help you do the following:

✔ Remember key points covered throughout this course.

✔ Fill out applications.

✔ Write a resume.

✔ Prepare for interviews.

Many activities contain page references to the *Data Minder* to help you easily transfer information to it. Follow your teacher's instructions in completing the *Data Minder*. Note that you cannot complete some of the *Data Minder* until you have covered material later in this workbook.

ACTIVITY

Your Educational Background

Data Minder *page 3*

List the schools you have attended on the following worksheet. Be sure to include your attendance dates.

WORKSHEET FOR SCHOOLS ATTENDED

Grade	Dates	School Name	Address, City, State, ZIP Code	Phone Number or E-mail Address
12th				
11th				
10th				
9th				
8th				
7th				
6th				
5th				
4th				
3rd				
2nd				
1st				
Kindergarten				

ACTIVITY

Your High School Courses

Data Minder *pages 4–5*

A large part of your life experience comes from school. Because employers will be interested in this experience, use it to support your ability to do the job.

HIGH SCHOOL CLASSES WORKSHEET

1. What courses, including vocational courses, have you taken in high school?

   _____

   _____

   _____

   _____

2. What types of jobs might these courses prepare you for?_____

   _____

   _____

   _____

3. List the most important things you learned to do in these courses:

   _____

   _____

   _____

   _____

4. What tools and equipment did you learn to use?_____

_____

_____

_____

_____

_____

5. Did you complete special projects related to these courses, such as a service-learning experience, a presentation, or a research paper? What skills did you develop by working on these projects?_____

_____

_____

_____

_____

_____

6. How can you use these courses after you complete high school?_____

_____

_____

_____

_____

_____

ACTIVITY

Your Extracurricular Activities

Data Minder *page 5*

Participation in sports, clubs, and other extracurricular activities can help show that you are a hard worker and have other skills.

EXTRACURRICULAR ACTIVITIES

List all the extracurricular activities that you have been involved in:

_____

_____

_____

_____

_____

_____

_____

_____

_____

_____

_____

_____

Select one activity you like most or that is most important to you, and complete the following worksheet. If you want to include more extracurricular activities, make copies of the worksheet or put the information on blank paper.

EXTRACURRICULAR ACTIVITY WORKSHEET

1. Activity:_____

2. Number of months or years involved, with dates:_____

   _____

3. Leadership role(s) you held:_____

   _____

   _____

4. Describe what you did in this activity:_____

   _____

   _____

   _____

5. List any special achievements and honors:_____

   _____

   _____

6. List the self-management, transferable, and job-related skills used in this activity that would be important to a future employer:

   _____

   _____

   _____

ACTIVITY

Your Other Training

Data Minder *page 6*

List any formal or informal training you received that might help prepare you for a job, college, the military, and other goals. Examples of such training are workshops, seminars, and self-study programs.

OTHER TRAINING WORKSHEET

1. School or program name:_____

   _____

2. Street address:_____

3. City, state, ZIP code:_____

4. Phone number: (   )_____E-mail:_____

5. Dates attended:_____

6. Type of education or training:_____

   _____

   _____

   _____

7. Type of certification, degree, or special diploma:_____

   _____

   _____

   _____

8. Job-related skills you learned: _____

_____

_____

_____

9. Tools, machinery, and equipment used in training: _____

_____

_____

_____

ACTIVITY

Your Work Experience

Data Minder *pages 8–13*

This activity collects information on jobs you have had. Include all part-time jobs, summer jobs, and internships here, even if you worked only for a short time. Also use the worksheets for unpaid volunteer or informal work, such as helping in the family business, mowing lawns, babysitting, or similar activities. You can count all of these things as "work." Start with your most recent job and work backward.

VOLUNTEER/PAID WORK EXPERIENCE WORKSHEET

Job 1

1. Name of organization:_____

2. Street address:_____

3. City, state, ZIP code:_____

4. Phone number: (   )_____

   E-mail:_____

5. Supervisor or person in charge:_____

6. Job title:_____

7. Starting date:_____ Ending date:_____

8. Starting date:_____ Ending date:_____

9. List your job duties and responsibilities:_____

   _____

   _____

   _____

---

10. List raises or promotions you received:_____

_____

11. Other recognition (such as positive evaluations) you received:_____

_____

12. Reasons for leaving the job:_____

_____

Job 2

1. Name of organization:_____

2. Street address:_____

3. City, state, ZIP code:_____

4. Phone number: (   )_____

    E-mail:_____

5. Supervisor or person in charge:_____

6. Job title:_____

7. Starting date:_____ Ending date:_____

8. Starting date:_____ Ending date:_____

9. List your job duties and responsibilities:_____

_____

_____

_____

_____

10. List raises or promotions you received:_____

_____

(continued)

(continued)

11. Other recognition (such as positive evaluations) you received:_____

_____

12. Reasons for leaving the job:_____

_____

Job 3

1. Name of organization:_____

2. Street address:_____

3. City, state, ZIP code:_____

4. Phone number: (   )_____

   E-mail:_____

5. Supervisor or person in charge:_____

6. Job title:_____

7. Starting date:_____ Ending date:_____

8. Starting date:_____ Ending date:_____

9. List your job duties and responsibilities:_____

_____

_____

_____

10. List raises or promotions you received:_____

_____

11. Other recognition (such as positive evaluations) you received:_____

_____

12. Reasons for leaving the job:_____

_____

Job 4

1. Name of organization:_____

2. Street address:_____

3. City, state, ZIP code:_____

4. Phone number: (   )_____

   E-mail:_____

5. Supervisor or person in charge:_____

6. Job title:_____

7. Starting date:_____ Ending date:_____

8. Starting date:_____ Ending date:_____

9. List your job duties and responsibilities:_____

_____

_____

_____

10. List raises or promotions you received:_____

_____

11. Other recognition (such as positive evaluations) you received:_____

_____

12. Reasons for leaving the job:_____

_____

(continued)

(continued)

Job 5

1. Name of organization: _____

2. Street address: _____

3. City, state, ZIP code: _____

4. Phone number: (   ) _____

    E-mail: _____

5. Supervisor or person in charge: _____

6. Job title: _____

7. Starting date: _____ Ending date: _____

8. Starting date: _____ Ending date: _____

9. List your job duties and responsibilities: _____

    _____

    _____

    _____

10. List raises or promotions you received: _____

    _____

11. Other recognition (such as positive evaluations) you received: _____

    _____

12. Reasons for leaving the job: _____

    _____

Job 6

1. Name of organization:_____

2. Street address:_____

3. City, state, ZIP code:_____

4. Phone number: (   )_____

   E-mail:_____

5. Supervisor or person in charge:_____

6. Job title:_____

7. Starting date:_____ Ending date:_____

8. Starting date:_____ Ending date:_____

9. List your job duties and responsibilities:_____

   _____

   _____

   _____

10. List raises or promotions you received:_____

    _____

11. Other recognition (such as positive evaluations) you received:_____

    _____

12. Reasons for leaving the job:_____

    _____

ACTIVITY

Your Professional Memberships, Hobbies, Honors, and Family Responsibilities

Data Minder *pages 14-15*

The activities you do outside of school and at home show that you have experience or a special interest in something. The same is true of awards and honors you've received.

You may not think that some of these activities can count as experience, but many employers consider them. These activities can be even more important if you have little paid work experience.

Think about the things you have done outside of school and at home that required responsibility, hard work, or special knowledge, or activities that you feel you did well. Also think about any awards or honors you've received.

OTHER EXPERIENCES WORKSHEET

1. **Professional memberships:** This includes memberships related to a job (such as a grocery store union) or chosen career field (such as the Future Teacher's Association). Be sure to list any leadership roles you held.

   _____

   _____

   _____

   _____

---

2. **Hobbies:** Give details about each hobby, emphasizing skills and accomplishments:_____

_____

_____

_____

_____

_____

_____

3. **Honors, awards, achievements:** Give details, including dates:

_____

_____

_____

_____

_____

_____

4. **Family responsibilities:** Give details and emphasize responsibilities and skills you used or learned:_____

_____

_____

_____

_____

_____

Select Your References

Many employers want to verify the points you have told them about yourself. They will ask you for the names of people who know you and your work. Following are the sources of the most common references.

Work References

These are people who can tell employers that you are likely to make a good worker. The best work references are usually the people who supervised you on paid or volunteer jobs. Other good choices are older coworkers, teachers, coaches, and leaders of any social or religious groups who know what kind of work you do. Most employers think that these are the best sources of information for determining the kind of worker you are.

Personal References

Personal references are people who know what you are like as a person and who have known you for at least two years. Most employers will not bother to contact a relative or friend about you. They know that these people like you but may not be able to give them information about your work skills. The best personal references include adult friends of your family, parents of your best friends, neighbors, and clergy.

Tips for References

Working with references is easier if you follow these tips:

✔ Always ask people if you can use them as references, and discuss what they will say about you.

✔ Tell your references the type of job you are looking for and the skills and experience you have to do it well.

✔ Be sure to list four or five people who will say only good things about you.

✔ Include both work and personal references.

✔ Do not use relatives or friends as references.

✔ Make sure your references can be reached easily by phone during the day. This is when most employers will call.

✔ Create a one-page list of references, as shown in the example on the next page.

When you are listing your references, use the following guidelines:

Information About the Reference	Example
Full name	Mr./Mrs./Miss/Ms. First Name Last Name
Job title or relationship to you	Vocational Instructor
Place of employment	Local School
Street address	000 Any Road
City, state, ZIP code	Anytown, Georgia 00001
Area code and home or work phone number	Work: (555) 555-0000
E-mail address (if available)	teacher@email.com

The following page shows one way that you can list references.

REFERENCES

for

ROBERT B. HIRED

Center each
reference

Mr. William Jones ——————— List the full name
Criminal Justice Instructor
Neighborhood Vocational School —— List the place of employment
7300 North Palmyra Road
Anytown, Ohio 00001
Work: (555) 555-1111

Rev. Frederick Smith
Pastor ————————— Include the job title or
Neighborhood Lutheran Church   relationship to you
745 Market Street
Anytown, Ohio 00001
Home: (555) 555-2222

Include at least three
references—both work and   Separate each reference with two
personal   or three blank lines

Mr. George Thomas
Guidance Counselor
Neighborhood High School
500 Educational Highway
Anytown, Ohio 00001
Work: (555) 555-3333
gthomas@dot.com ——————— Include an e-mail address if available

Do not number references

Mrs. Jane Doe
Office Manager
Steel Valley Crane Company
42 Main Street
Anytown, Ohio 00001
Work: (555) 555-4444 —————— List the area code and a daytime
Home: (555) 555-5555   phone number
steelvalley@net.com

ACTIVITY

Gather Information on Your References

Data Minder *pages 16–19*

In the spaces below, list the persons you might use as your work and personal references.

WORK REFERENCES WORKSHEET

Name:_____

Job title:_____

Place of employment:_____

Street address:_____

City, state, ZIP code:_____

Phone number: (   )_____

E-mail address:_____

Name:_____

Job title:_____

Place of employment:_____

Street address:_____

City, state, ZIP code:_____

Phone number: (   )_____

E-mail address:_____

Name:_____

Job title:_____

Place of employment:_____

Street address:_____

City, state, ZIP code:_____

Phone number: (   )_____

E-mail address:_____

PERSONAL REFERENCES WORKSHEET

Name:_____

Job title:_____

Place of employment:_____

Street address:_____

City, state, ZIP code:_____

Phone number: (   )_____

E-mail address:_____

Name:_____

Job title:_____

Place of employment:_____

Street address:_____

City, state, ZIP code:_____

Phone number: (   )_____

E-mail address:_____

Name:_____

Job title:_____

Place of employment:_____

Street address:_____

City, state, ZIP code:_____

Phone number: (   )_____

E-mail address:_____

Use This Information to Your Advantage

As you will learn in Chapter 11, you have only a few minutes to make a good impression in an interview. You will have to tell employers about the skills and experiences that make you a good person for the job. This makes it important that you know, in advance, the most important details to tell employers about yourself. You probably have more positive things to tell them than you realize. We hope this chapter helps.

Chapter 5

Use the JIST Card®

A JIST Card is a mini-resume that you can use in various ways during your job search. In this chapter, you will learn how to write and use a JIST Card effectively.

Basic Information About You

Although a JIST Card is usually only three-by-five inches, it will include the information that most employers need to know about you.

Read the sample JIST Card that follows. Imagine that you are an employer who hires people with similar skills. Your "company" may or may not have a job opening at this time. Review the information on the card and let yourself react naturally to what you feel about this potential employee.

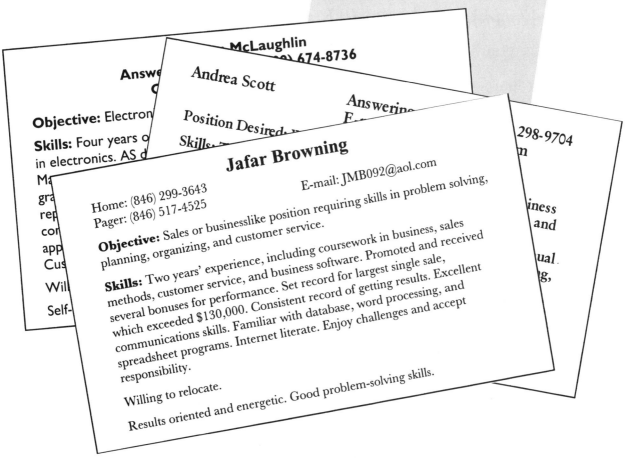

McLaughlin
674-8736

Andrea Scott

Objective: Electron

Skills: Four years o
in electronics. AS d

Position Desired

Skills

Answering

Jafar Browning

Home: (846) 299-3643
Pager: (846) 517-4525

E-mail: JMB092@aol.com

Objective: Sales or businesslike position requiring skills in problem solving, planning, organizing, and customer service.

Skills: Two years' experience, including coursework in business, sales methods, customer service, and business software. Promoted and received several bonuses for performance. Set record for largest single sale, which exceeded $130,000. Consistent record of getting results. Excellent communications skills. Familiar with database, word processing, and spreadsheet programs. Internet literate. Enjoy challenges and accept responsibility.

Willing to relocate.

Results oriented and energetic. Good problem-solving skills.

298-9704

John Kijek
Home: (876) 232-9213
Pager: (876) 637-6643
E-mail: jkijek@net.com

Position desired: Administrative assistant

Skills: Over two years' work experience, including one year in a full-time training program. Familiar with spreadsheet programs, database programs, computerized accounting systems, Internet use, and most standard computer operations. Word process at 55 wpm using good format and grammar. Have trained three staff members in a retail environment and helped increase sales more than 12%. Good writing and language skills. I work well independently and as part of a team.

Will relocate.

Honest, reliable, hard working, and well organized.

YOUR TURN

How Would You React to a JIST Card?

Think carefully and then write your answers to the following questions.

1. If you were an employer, how would you feel about the person whose JIST Card you just read? _____

   _____

   _____

   _____

   _____

   _____

   _____

2. Would you interview this person if you had an opening? _____

Although JIST Cards appear to give very little information, most employers feel positive about them. Many employers would give this applicant an interview if they had an opening. They are that impressed!

TIP In Chapter 3, you identified the self-management, transferable, and job-related skills that you felt were most important for a job, and you supported each skill with an example. These skills and examples will be used in developing your own JIST Card.

Some Ways You Can Use a JIST Card

- ✔ Attach one to your application or resume.

- ✔ Present one as your business card before or after an interview.

- ✔ Leave one or more with your references.

- ✔ Give several to each of your friends, relatives, and others who might help you in your job search. Ask them to pass your JIST Card on to others who might know of an opening.

- ✔ Leave one with employers when you are refused an application or an interview. (It could help them change their minds!)

- ✔ Enclose one in a thank-you note following an interview or with other job search correspondence.

- ✔ Include one as an e-mail attachment or as part of the e-mail text.

YOUR TURN

Other Uses of a JIST Card

Write any other ideas for the use of your JIST Card here:_____

_____

_____

_____

_____

_____

Anatomy of a JIST Card

JIST Cards are more complicated than they first appear. Look over the various parts of a JIST Card in the following sample. It will help you learn how to create your own card.

John Kijek
Home: (876) 232-9213 ⎤
Pager: (876) 637-6643 ⎦ ——— Two phone numbers
E-mail: jkijek@net.com ——— E-mail address

Position desired: Administrative assistant ——— Position

Experience, education, and training   Job-related skills and results

Skills: Over two years' work experience, including one year in a full-time training program. Familiar with spreadsheet programs, database programs, computerized accounting systems, Internet use, and most standard computer operations. Word process at 55 wpm using good format and grammar. Have trained three staff members in a retail environment and helped increase sales more than 12%. Good writing and language skills. I work well independently and as part of a team.

Will relocate. ——— Special conditions   Transferable skills

Honest, reliable, hard working, and well organized.

Good-worker traits and self-management skills

3×5 white or light-color card

Tips for Writing Your JIST Card

Use the following tips as you write your JIST Card:

✔ **Name:** Use your formal name. Avoid nicknames.

✔ **Phone number:** An employer will most likely contact you by phone or e-mail. If you're not able to answer your home phone during the day (or if you don't have a phone), ask a reliable friend or relative to take messages. Another option is to get voicemail or an answering machine. Just make sure your message sounds professional. Many JIST Cards include a second phone number to increase the chance of an employer reaching you. This may be a pager number, a cell phone number, or some other alternative phone number.

✔ **E-mail address:** Include your e-mail address if you have one. Keep in mind that free e-mail accounts are available through a variety of sources. If you don't have a computer, you can access your account at libraries and schools with Internet connections.

✔ **Position/job objective:** If your job objective is too specific, it will limit the jobs for which you may be considered. Instead, use a job objective that allows you to be considered for more positions, yet is not too general.

Use an objective that allows you to be considered for several jobs.

✔ **Skills:** Skills can be reflected in several ways:

* **Education and experience:** Take credit for everything you've done. Everything can count, including education, training, paid employment, related volunteer work, hobbies, and other informal experience. Add up the total amount of time you have spent gaining this experience. For example, if you spent the past four summers babysitting for the neighbors during the day, you have one year of full-time child care work experience.

* **Job-related skills and results:** Mention the things you can do specific to the job, such as using special tools or computers. Emphasize accomplishments and use numbers (such as percentage of sales or profits increased, number of units produced, and so on).

* **Transferable skills:** Mention ones that are important to the job and that you do well. Refer to the skills checklists in Chapter 3. Use examples where possible.

* **Self-management skills:** Include at least three of your strongest self-management skills. Select the ones from your checklist in Chapter 3 that seem important for this job.

✔ **Special conditions:** This is an optional section. Use it to list special advantages you offer that don't fit elsewhere.

Sample JIST Cards

Look over the sample JIST Cards that follow for ideas for your own.

Jonn Scott
Home: (219) 298-9704
E-mail: jscott@hotmail.com

Position: Retail sales

Two years' work experience plus two years' education in distributive education and marketing. Experience in fast-paced environment serving as many as 1,200 customers per day with weekly sales of more than $24,000. Familiar with retail display, purchasing, sales recording, selling techniques, and supervision of others. Excellent interpersonal and customer service skills.

Available full time. Will work weekends and evenings.

Results oriented, reliable, professional.

Note: Jonn's work experience was at a McDonald's and a senior-year co-op job. His education was in his high school business program.

Lisa Marie Marrin
Home: (213) 432-8064 Pager: (212) 876-9487
E-mail: lmarrin@webcast.net

Position: Hotel management

Two years of experience in sales, customer service, and catering for a 300-room hotel. Courses in business, marketing, computer skills, and distributive education. Organized catering events for groups as large as 200 and suggested improvements in registration procedures that saved more than $10,000 per year in personnel costs. Have been commended for improving staff productivity and courtesy. I approach my work with industry, imagination, and creative problem-solving skills.

Prefer full-time work with promotion potential.

Enthusiastic, well-organized, detail oriented.

Note: Lisa Marie had worked for the hotel on weekends and during summers while going to high school. She took several business and computer courses and plans to continue to work in the hospitality industry to pay her way through college.

Rafael Mendez
Message: (602) 257-6643   E-mail: rafaelmen@gmail.net

Objective: Computer support specialist or Internet site developer

One year of work experience plus extensive knowledge of computer hardware and software. Can troubleshoot and repair all major PC computers and peripherals, including business "rack" systems. Familiar with many software packages, including major word processing, database, spreadsheet, graphic design, and utility programs. Have set up, updated, trained, and supported many new and experienced PC users. Have also designed and managed more than 10 Web sites, the largest with more than 2,000 pages and 800,000 hits per year. Efficient at managing many priorities and heavy workloads.

Willing to work long hours in an informal work environment.

Good people skills, able to learn quickly, reliable.

Note: All of Rafael's computer skills are self-taught. He has been involved with computers for years and spends much of his free time working with hardware and software and with other computer enthusiasts. He has earned enough from his freelance Web design work to buy his car and save for more formal education.

Sandy Zaremba

Home: (512) 232-7608
Message: (512) 234-7465
E-mail: SandraZ@organizedoffice.com

Position: General office/clerical

More than one-and-a-half years of work experience, plus one year of training in office practices. Type 55 wpm; trained in word processing operations; post general ledger; handle payables, receivables, and most computerized accounting tasks. Good interpersonal skills. Can meet deadlines and handle pressure well.

Willing to work any hours.

Organized, honest, reliable, and hard working.

Note: Sandy got her experience as a volunteer in her church business office and after school in a small bookkeeping firm. She also took some high school computer and office skills classes.

Maria Smith

Home: (888) 777-9999
E-mail: msmith@mail.com

Position: Office support staff

Qualifications: Graduating from high school in June XXXX. Focusing on academic and business courses, including accounting, keyboarding, computer literacy, and exploratory business. Able to produce various Office documents. Capable of using personal computer, transcriber, and software such as Microsoft Office, PageMaker, and Web browsers. Proficient in keeping records and in using correct grammar, spelling, and punctuation. Efficient in following instructions and meeting deadlines.

Available for part-time work, weekdays after noon.

Organized — Dependable — Accurate — Professional

Note: Marie will be graduating from high school in less than a year. Although she has not had formal work experience, her high school business courses and self-taught software skills make her marketable for a good part-time job now.

> "We are what we repeatedly do. Excellence, then, is not an act, but a habit."
>
> *Aristotle*

ACTIVITY

Your Practice JIST Card

Use the following worksheet to write a first draft of your JIST Card. You may want to make rough drafts of some sections on separate sheets of paper. When your information is right, you can transfer it to this worksheet.

JIST CARD FIRST DRAFT WORKSHEET

Name:_____

Home phone number:_____

Alternative phone number:_____

E-mail address:_____

Position desired:_____

_____

Education and training:_____

_____

_____

_____

_____

Job-related experience:_____

_____

_____

_____

_____

(continued)

(continued)

Job-related skills and results statement:_____

_____

_____

_____

_____

Transferable skills statement:_____

_____

_____

_____

_____

_____

Special conditions (optional):_____

_____

_____

_____

Good-worker traits and self-management skills:_____

_____

_____

_____

_____

_____

_____

_____

ACTIVITY

Your Final JIST Card

Data Minder *pages 20–21*

Now use the information from the worksheet you just completed to write your JIST Card in the spaces that follow. Modify the wording as needed.

JIST CARD FINAL DRAFT WORKSHEET

(Name:)
_____

Home phone number:_____

Alternative phone number:_____

E-mail address:_____

Position desired: _____

Experience, education, and training _____

Skills: Over _____ months/years of experience in _____,

plus training/courses in _____ and _____.

Skilled in _____ , _____ , _____ , _____ and _____.

Able to _____ , _____ , _____ , _____ and _____.

I have done _____ , _____ , _____ and _____.

2 transferable skills
I am also _____ and _____.

Available: _____.

_____ , _____ , _____ , _____.

10–12 related skills and results

4 self-management skills

Special conditions

Tips for Producing Your JIST Card

After you have written your JIST Card, you will want to produce enough to give to others. The following tips can help you with that process.

- ✔ Make sure your JIST Card has no grammar or spelling errors. Also check the phone numbers and e-mail addresses for accuracy.

- ✔ Make arrangements to have your card professionally produced on index (heavy) weight paper. A good-quality photocopy machine can often give you what you need. You can also create and print out your cards on a personal computer and laser printer.

- ✔ Discuss different ways to format your card. Experiment, be creative, and make yours look attractive and professional.

- ✔ Consider using a soft, light paper color, such as white, ivory, beige, cream, or gray.

- ✔ Most JIST Cards are approximately three-by-five inches, but you can be a bit creative with yours if you want to. Some people have used a business-card size or a folded card to make theirs stand out.

- ✔ Be sure to see and approve the final draft before the printer completes your order.

- ✔ Print at least 50 to 100 cards so that you can give them out freely to employers and people you know.

- ✔ Format your JIST Card so that you can attach it to an e-mail, with another text-only version that you can include in the e-mail itself.

JIST Cards can be effective in helping you find job leads, but they won't work unless you use them. So plan on getting as many as you can into the hands of employers, friends, relatives, and others.

Chapter 6

Find Job Leads

For some people, finding a job is not too hard. Young people can find entry-level jobs (in restaurants and fast-food places, for example) quite easily. But finding a really good job is often more difficult. The competition is greater. More people with greater education, training, or experience are applying for the desirable jobs. This chapter covers various job search techniques that will give you the competitive edge in getting both entry-level and career-oriented jobs.

Most employers hire people they already know.

ACTIVITY

How Do People Find Jobs?

The U.S. Department of Labor conducts a regular survey of unemployed people actively looking for work. These methods are listed next. Some of the methods, such as contacting an employer directly or sending out resumes, include those using the Internet. In the spaces that follow, guess what percentage of job seekers used each method. Because most job seekers use more than one method, the total will be more than 100 percent.

PERCENTAGES OF METHODS USED TO FIND JOBS

1. Contacted employers directly_____

2. Sent out resumes or filled out applications_____

3. Contacted the public employment agency_____

4. Placed or answered help-wanted ads_____

5. Contacted friends or relatives_____

6. Contacted private employment agency_____

7. Contacted school employment center_____

8. Checked union or professional registers_____

9. Used other active job search methods_____

Compare your guesses with others in the class, and then look up the answers at the end of this chapter. Discuss your guesses and the actual percentages in class.

Some Search Methods Work Better Than Others to Find Job Leads

The survey shows that most people use more than one job search technique. For example, one person might read want ads, fill out applications, and ask friends for job leads. Others might send out resumes, contact everyone they know from professional contacts, and sign up at employment agencies.

But the survey covered only nine job search methods and asked only whether the job seeker did or did not use each method. The survey did not cover Internet job searches, and it didn't ask whether a method actually worked in getting job offers.

Unfortunately, there hasn't been much recent research on the effectiveness of various job search methods. Most of what we know is based on older research and the observations of people who work with job seekers. I'll share what we do know about the effectiveness of job search methods in the content that follows.

Get the Most Out of Less Effective Job Search Methods

The truth is that every job search method works for someone. But experience and research show that some methods are more effective than others. Your task in the job search is to spend more of your time using more effective methods—and increase the effectiveness of all the methods you use.

So let's start by looking at some traditional job search methods and how you can increase their effectiveness. Only about one-third of all job seekers get their jobs using these methods, but you should still consider using them.

 TIP Almost everyone finds a job eventually, so your objective should be to find a good job in less time. The job search methods we emphasize in this book will help you do just that.

Newspaper and Internet Help-Wanted Ads

Most jobs are never advertised, and only about 15 percent of all people get their jobs through the want ads. Everyone who reads the paper knows about these openings, so competition is fierce for the few advertised jobs.

The Internet also lists many job openings. But, as happens with newspaper ads, enormous numbers of people view these postings. People do get jobs this way, though, so go ahead and apply for them. Just be sure to spend most of your time using more effective methods.

Internet job seeking is covered in more detail later in this chapter.

Employment Applications

Most employers require job seekers to complete an application form. Applications are designed to collect negative information, and employers use applications to screen people out. If, for example, your training or work history is not the best, you're not likely to get an interview, even if you can do the job.

Completing applications is a more effective approach for young and entry-level job seekers. That's because there's a shortage of workers for the relatively low-paying jobs that less experienced job seekers typically seek. As a result, when trying to fill those positions, employers are more willing to accept a lack of experience or job skills.

Even so, you will get better results by filling out the application, if asked to do so, and then requesting an interview with the person in charge.

When you complete an application, make it neat and error-free, and do not include anything that could get you screened out. If necessary, leave a problem section blank. You can always explain it after you get an interview. A separate chapter on applications will cover them in more detail.

Employment Agencies

There are three types of employment agencies. One is operated by the government and is free. The others are run as for-profit businesses that charge a fee either to you or an employer. Here are the advantages and disadvantages of using each.

The Government Employment Service and One-Stop Centers

Each state has a network of local offices to pay unemployment compensation, provide job leads, and offer other services at no charge to you or to employers. The service's name varies by state. It may be called "Job Service," "Department of Labor," "Unemployment Office," "Workforce Development," or another name.

Many states also have "One-Stop Centers" that provide employment counseling, reference books, computerized career information, job listings, and other resources.

We do not suggest that you should *never* use less effective techniques. Some people get good jobs using the worst of methods, and that's fine. We do suggest that you use a *variety* of methods, spending most of your time using techniques that work best for most people.

Whatever job search method that works is good.

The Internet site at www.doleta.gov/uses gives information on the programs provided by the government employment service, plus links to other useful sites. Another Internet site, America's Job Bank at www.ajb.dni.us, allows visitors to see all jobs listed with the government employment service and to search for jobs by region and other criteria.

The government employment service lists only 5 to 10 percent of the available openings nationally, and only about 6 percent of all job seekers get their jobs there. Even so, visit your local office early in your job search. Find out if you qualify for unemployment compensation and learn more about its services. Look into the government employment service. The price is right.

Private Employment Agencies

Private employment agencies are businesses that charge a fee either to you or to the employer who hires you. Fees can be from less than one month's pay to 15 percent or more of your annual salary. You will often see these agencies' ads in the help-wanted section of the newspaper. Many have Web sites.

Be careful about using fee-based employment agencies. Recent research indicates that more people use and benefit from fee-based agencies than in the past. However, relatively few people who register with private agencies get a job through them.

If you use a private employment agency, ask for interviews with employers who will pay the agency's fee. Do not sign an exclusive agreement or be pressured into accepting a job, and continue to actively look for your own leads. You can find these agencies in the phone book's yellow pages. A government-run Web site at www.ajb.dni.us also lists many of them.

Temporary Agencies

Temporary agencies offer jobs lasting from several days to many months. They charge the employer a fee per hour, and then they pay you a bit less and keep the difference. You pay no direct fee to the agency. Many private employment agencies now provide temporary jobs, too.

Temp agencies have grown rapidly for good reason. They give employers short-term help, and employers often use them to find people they may want to hire later.

School and Employment Services

Contacting a school employment center is one of the job search methods included in the survey presented earlier. Only a small percentage of respondents used this option. This is probably because few had the service available to them. Find out about the employment services at your school. Some schools provide free career counseling, resume-writing help, referrals to job openings, career interest tests, reference materials, and other services.

In addition to school employment centers, special career programs work with veterans, people with disabilities, welfare recipients, union members, professional groups, and many others. Just knowing about these services will be valuable for you in the future.

Human Resources Departments

Few people get hired by someone in a human resources department. The human resources department's job is to screen you out. Be cooperative with human resources staff, but try to go directly to the person who is most likely to supervise you, even if no opening exists right now. Remember that most smaller organizations don't even have a human resources office—only the larger ones do.

Mailed Resumes and Internet Postings

Many job search "experts" used to suggest that sending out lots of resumes was a great technique. That advice probably helped sell their resume books, but mailing resumes to people you do not know has never been an effective approach. Every so often this works, but a 95-percent failure rate and few interviews continue to be the more common outcomes.

Although mailing your resume to strangers doesn't make much sense, posting it on the Internet might for the following reasons:

✔ It doesn't take much time.

✔ Many employers can find your resume there.

Still, job searching on the Internet has its limitations, just like other methods do.

TIP Job seekers should have a good resume. How you use your resume to get results is the issue. This book presents electronic resumes in more detail later and provides tips on using the Internet throughout.

The Two Job Search Methods That Work Best

The fact is that most jobs are not advertised. So how do *you* find them? The same way about two-thirds of all job seekers do—networking with people you know (which we call making *warm contacts*) and directly contacting employers (which we call making *cold contacts*). Both of these methods are based on the job search rule that you should know above all others:

TIP Don't wait until a job is "open" before you contact the employer!

Employers fill most jobs with people they meet before a job is formally "open." So the trick is to meet people who can hire you before a job is formally available. Instead of asking, "Do you have any jobs open?", say, "I realize you may not have any openings now, but I would still like to talk to you about the possibility of future openings."

This simple change in how you approach the job search can make an enormous difference in your getting interviews while others wait for jobs to be advertised. Others remain unemployed, whereas you get interviews and job offers. Here are some details on how to do this most effectively.

It's true. You have to know someone to get a job. We have found, though, that you can quickly get to know all sorts of new people if you go about it right. One of them often turns out to be someone whom you need.

Most Effective Job Search Method #1: Develop a Network of People You Know (Warm Contacts)

Only 14 percent of job seekers ask their friends or relatives for job leads. But one study found that 40 percent of all people located their jobs through a lead provided by a friend, a relative, or an acquaintance. This means that asking their help is more effective than any other job search method. Because you already know these people, we call them *warm contacts*. Even if they don't know of a job opening for you, they will often give you names of other people they know who might help. Developing these new contacts is called *networking*. The next activity shows you how it works.

ACTIVITY

Establish Warm Contacts

Before you can develop your network, you need to think about the people you know.

1. **Develop a list of all the groups of people you know:** Begin with your friends and relatives. Then think of other groups of people with whom you have something in common. Examples are people you used to work with, people who went to your school, people in your social or sports groups, former employers, friends' parents, and members of your religious group.

GROUPS OF PEOPLE YOU KNOW WORKSHEET

Group	Number of People in This Group	Group	Number of People in This Group
Friends		Former employers	
Relatives		Former coworkers	
Neighbors		People I went to school with	
Friends of parents		Former teachers	
Members of my church or religious group		Members of sports or hobby groups	
People who sell me things (insurance agent, real estate agent, landlord, and so on)		People who provide me with services (hair stylist, counselor, mechanic, and so on)	
Write in other groups here:			

2. **Write a separate list of the people you know in each group:** Some lists, such as a list of your friends, may be quite long. For other lists, you may not know the names of everyone in the group. Examples are all the people who go to your church or people who graduated from your school in years past. You can get these names later. Just keep in mind that almost all these people will be willing to help you in your job search.

The worksheet that follows will help you list the people from one of your groups in an organized way. Complete this worksheet for that group, and use additional sheets for other groups. Be sure to include a label describing each group. We suggest that you begin by listing your friends and relatives.

NETWORK CONTACT WORKSHEET

Group 1: _____

Name	Phone Number	E-mail Address

(continued)

(continued)

3. **Contact people:** Start with your friends and relatives. Call them and explain that you are looking for a job and need their help. Be as clear as possible about what you are looking for and what your skills and qualifications are. Look at your JIST Card from Chapter 5 and the phone script in Chapter 7 for presentation ideas.

Job seeking is a contact sport.

4. **Ask for leads:** Some of the people you contact may know of a job opening that's just right for you. If so, get the details and get right on it! More than likely, however, they will not know of an opening, so here are three magic questions you should ask:

   * Do you know of any employers who may have an opening for someone with my skills?

     If no, then ask:

   * Do you know of someone else who might know of such an opening?

     If yes, get that person's name and phone number or e-mail address and ask for another name.

     If no, then ask:

   * Do you know someone who knows lots of people? If all else fails, this will usually get you a name.

5. **Keep records:** Keep a record of all your contacts. Simple 3×5–inch index cards are useful for recording important information, and they are easy to organize. Use the Job Lead Card example on the next page as a model.

6. **Follow up:** Call the people whom your contacts suggest and repeat steps 3, 4, and 5. For each original contact, you can extend your network of acquaintances by hundreds of people. It will be like the following illustration. Eventually, one of these people will hire you or refer you to someone who will!

Job Lead Card

Organization: _Mutual Health Insurance_

Contact person: _Anna Tomey_

Phone number: _(555) 555-2211_

Source of lead: _Aunt Ruth_

Notes: _4/10 called. Anna on vacation. Call back 4/15._
4/15 Interview set 4/20 at 1:30. 4/20 Anna showed
me around. They use the same computers we used in
school. Sent thank-you note and JIST Card. Call
back 5/1. 5/1 Second interview 5/8 at 9 a.m.

Person You Know

Fred   Susan

Networking: One Person Refers You to Two Others

Tips for Following Up

To strengthen your network, use the following tips for following up on warm contacts:

✔ Keep a record of all your networking contacts.

✔ Always complete a follow-up card for each contact.

✔ Have plenty of index cards on hand.

✔ Be pleasant and professional in all contacts.

✔ Within 24 hours, send a thank-you note or e-mail to each person you contact.

✔ Include a copy of your JIST Card in all correspondence.

✔ Get a card file box (available at office supply stores) and file your job lead cards under the date you want to follow up. Or use an electronic contact manager or scheduler to keep track of when to follow up.

Most Effective Job Search Method #2: Contact Employers Directly (Cold Contacts)

It takes more courage, but making direct contact with employers is an effective job search technique. We call these *cold contacts* because people you don't know in advance will need to warm up to your inquiries. Two basic techniques for making cold contacts follow.

About two out of three job seekers contact employers directly during their job search, making this the most used job search method. Other research shows that about one-third of all job seekers get their jobs this way. But many more job seekers would get their jobs through direct contacts with employers if they changed what they did. For example, instead of completing an application or applying through an employer's Web site, we encourage you to use more active methods.

Because most jobs are not advertised, one effective way to find openings is to call employers who might need a person with your skills. The yellow pages is a good source of places to call. Another source is the Internet, which provides a variety of ways to find places to call. For example, yellow pages listings are available online for any geographic area of the country. Many businesses have Web sites that provide company information and contact numbers. Also, America's

Contacting an employer directly is an effective job search technique.

Career InfoNet at www.acinet.org is sponsored by the U.S. government and gives contact information for individual employers. Employers are organized by industry and location.

After you locate an organization that may need your skills, call it and ask for the person in charge. Then ask that person if you can come in for an interview. You will learn more about how to do this later in this workbook.

You can also just walk in and ask to speak to the person in charge. This is particularly effective in small businesses but works surprisingly well in larger ones, too. Remember: You want an interview even if no openings exist now.

TIP If your timing is inconvenient, ask for a better time to come back for an interview. It works!

Pay Attention to Small Businesses

About two out of three people now work in smaller businesses—those with 250 or fewer workers. Whereas the largest corporations have reduced their number of employees, small businesses have been creating as many as 80 percent of all new jobs. Many opportunities exist to obtain training and to advance in smaller organizations. Many do not even have human resources departments, so nontraditional job search techniques are particularly effective with them.

Where People Work

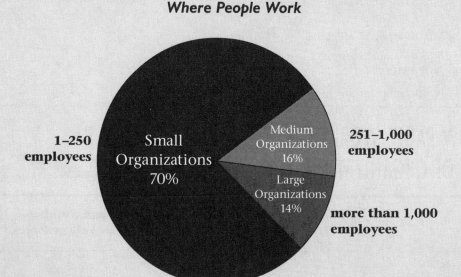

ACTIVITY

Use the Yellow Pages

1. Find the index section in the current yellow pages. This is usually in the front of the book. It lists the various types of businesses and other organizations within each area. If you are using a computer for this activity, go to www.yellowpages.com and browse the index.

2. Begin looking at the listings and ask yourself this question:

   Could this type of organization possibly use a person with my skills?

   (It will help if you have a job objective here, such as "administrative assistant" or "auto mechanic.")

3. On the worksheet that follows, list at least 10 types of organizations from the yellow pages index that might hire people with your skills. Record these 10 types of organizations.

4. For each organization, list the page number in the yellow pages where you could look up more information.

5. Decide how interested you are in working for this type of organization and mark the entry with one of the following codes:

   1 = Very interested

   2 = Somewhat interested

   3 = Not interested

YELLOW PAGES WORKSHEET I: TYPES OF ORGANIZATIONS

Type of Organization	Page Number in Yellow Pages	Rank
1.		
2.		
3.		

Type of Organization	Page Number in Yellow Pages	Rank
4.		
5.		
6.		
7.		
8.		
9.		
10.		

6. Continue looking at listings in the yellow pages index. For each listing, ask the same question:

Could this type of organization possibly use a person with my skills?

If you want to keep track of the organizations that interest you, list them on a separate piece of paper. Doing so will help you discover many employers that you would normally overlook.

ACTIVITY

List Specific Organizations

1. Turn to the yellow pages section for each type of organization and list the specific companies or organizations there. These organizations are hot prospects for you to contact in your job search.

   The Yellow Pages Worksheet 2 gives you an example of how you can organize the contact information. You can get the organization's e-mail or Web site address by entering the organization name in your Internet browser or just calling and asking.

2. Make additional copies of the worksheet as needed.

YELLOW PAGES WORKSHEET 2: SPECIFIC ORGANIZATIONS

Group 1. Yellow Pages Index Listing:			Group 2. Yellow Pages Index Listing:		
Specific Organization	Phone Number	E-mail	Specific Organization	Phone Number	E-mail

TIP For each contact, follow up with a thank-you note or e-mail and include your JIST Card.

Note: In Chapter 7, you will learn how to contact each organization and ask for an interview. In this way, you can generate many job leads from the hidden job market.

Use the Internet for Job Leads

The Internet has limitations as a job search tool. Although many have used it to get job leads, it has not worked well for far more. Too many assume that they can simply add their resume to resume databases, and employers will line up to hire them. Just as with the older approach of sending out lots of resumes, good things sometimes happen, but not often.

We recommend two points of view that apply to all job search methods, including the Internet:

✔ It is unwise to rely on just one or two methods of conducting your job search.

✔ It is essential that you use an active rather than a passive approach in your job search.

Ways to Increase Your Internet Effectiveness

We encourage you to use the Internet in your job search but suggest that you use it along with other techniques, including direct contacts with employers. The following suggestions can increase the effectiveness of using the Internet in your job search:

✔ **Be as specific as possible in identifying the job you seek:** This is important in using any job search method and even more so in looking for jobs on the Internet. The Internet is enormous, so it is essential to be as focused as possible in what you are searching for. Narrow your job title or titles to be as specific as possible. Limit your search to specific industries or areas of specialization.

✔ **Have reasonable expectations:** Success on the Internet is more likely if you understand its limitations. For example, employers trying to find someone with skills in high demand, such as network engineers or nurses, are more likely to use the Internet to recruit job candidates.

✔ **Limit your geographic options:** If you don't want to move, or you would move but only to certain areas, state this preference on your resume and restrict your search to those areas. Many Internet sites allow you to view only those jobs that meet your location criteria.

✔ **Create an electronic resume:** With few exceptions, resumes submitted on the Internet end up as simple text files with no graphics elements. Employers search databases of many resumes for those that include key words or meet other searchable criteria. So create a simple text resume for Internet use and include on it words likely to be used by employers searching for someone with your abilities.

✔ **Get your resume into the major resume databases:** Most Internet employment sites let you add your resume for free, and then they charge employers to advertise openings or to search for candidates. These easy-to-use sites often provide all sorts of useful information for job seekers.

✔ **Make direct contacts:** Visit Web sites of organizations that interest you and learn more about them. Some will post openings, allow you to apply online, or even provide access to staff who can answer your questions. Even if they don't, you can always e-mail a request for the name of the person in charge of the work that interests you and then communicate with that person directly.

✔ **Network:** You can network online, too, finding names and e-mail addresses of potential employer contacts or of other people who might know someone with job openings. Look at interest groups, professional association sites, alumni sites, chat rooms, and employer sites. These are just some of the many creative ways to network and interact with people via the Internet.

You could spend weeks and months browsing the Internet. Your task is to get a job, not to wander the Web endlessly.

Useful Internet Sites

Thousands of Internet sites provide information on careers or education. Many have links to other sites that they recommend. Service providers such as America Online (www.aol.com) and the MSN (www.msn.com) have career information and job listings, plus links to other sites. Larger portal sites offer links to recommended career-related sites. Google (www.google.com), and Yahoo! (www.yahoo.com) are just a few of these portals. Here are some major career-specific sites to get you started:

✔ **www.rileyguide.com:** Good information, plus links to many other sites.

✔ **www.ajb.dni.us:** America's Job Bank, a government site that provides job openings in all areas of the country.

✔ **www.jist.com:** Provides free job search information and links to other sites.

✔ **www.monster.com:** The largest commercial resume posting and advertised job opening site.

✔ **CareerOINK.com:** Provides information on thousands of job titles and links to other sites.

Answers to "How Do People Find Jobs?"

The following figures show the percentage of people who used each of the major job search methods listed in the survey of unemployed workers. These are the correct answers to the first activity in this chapter. How close were your answers?

1. 65 percent contacted employers directly.

2. 48 percent sent out resumes or filled out applications.

3. 20 percent contacted the public employment agency.

4. 15 percent placed or answered help-wanted ads.

5. 14 percent contacted friends or relatives.

6. 7 percent contacted a private employment agency.

7. 2 percent contacted a school placement center.

8. 2 percent checked union or professional registers.

9. 4 percent used other miscellaneous methods.

Source: U.S. Department of Labor, Current Population Survey

> "Great ability develops and reveals itself increasingly with every new assignment."
>
> Baltasar Gracian

Chapter 7

Make Direct Contacts with Employers

Remember that most jobs are never advertised. They are found in the hidden job market. As explained in Chapter 6, making cold contacts with employers is an effective way to find these hidden jobs. You can make these cold contacts with employers by doing the following:

✔ E-mailing or calling them on the phone

✔ Visiting them in person

This chapter covers ways to make direct contact with an employer and then follow up to get an interview. These methods are considered cold contacts because you do not know the employers you will contact.

66*When you are content to be simply yourself and don't compare or compete, everybody will respect you.*99

Lao-Tzu

Contact Employers by Telephone

Using the telephone in your job search offers many advantages:

✔ **Saves time and money:** Most people can call 10 to 20 employers in one hour. You might spend a whole day contacting the same number of employers in person. You also save transportation money and related costs.

✔ **Creates new opportunities:** By calling potential employers directly, you can often uncover job openings long before they will be advertised. An employer may even create a job for you because you sound like the right person with the right skills.

✔ **Makes a positive impression:** Good telephone skills can create a positive impression. This will give you the edge over those who simply fill out an application or send in a resume. You also appear more assertive.

✔ **Gets directly to the hiring authority:** Using the phone makes it much easier to get directly to the person who is most likely to supervise someone with your skills. It is much more effective than filling out applications or sending in resumes.

✔ **Gets results:** People who use the telephone well can get many more interviews than people using traditional methods. Many will also get job offers sooner.

You Can Do It!

Many people find it hard to make phone calls to employers they don't know. They are afraid of being rejected. But preparation can make it much easier. The two most important things to do are the following:

✔ Know what you are going to say in advance.

✔ Practice your telephone presentation by yourself and with others until you feel prepared to make calls to employers.

A Sample Telephone Script

Your JIST Card, with just a few changes, can form the basis for an effective telephone script. Here is an example, based on a JIST Card presented in Chapter 5:

May I speak to the person in charge of your business office?

> *Hello, my name is Maria Smith, and I'm interested in office support work. I'll be graduating from high school in June and have been focusing on academic and business courses, including accounting, keyboarding, computer literacy, and exploratory business. From these courses, I have hands-on experience in producing various office documents and doing basic accounting tasks, including spreadsheets.*
>
> *I can keep accurate records, and I am familiar with various software products, including Microsoft Office, PageMaker, and Web browsers. I think you will find me to be organized, dependable, and professional.*

When may I come in for an interview?

How Does It Sound to You?

If you were an employer, how would you feel about someone saying the sample script to you on the phone? Would you give this person an interview?

The telephone script based on your JIST Card is a powerful tool.

When asked this same question, most employers say they would interview this person. They were interested enough in what the person said to consider him or her for an opening—if they did not have one right away! From beginning to end, this phone script takes less than 30 seconds to say out loud. Yet many employers have granted interviews on just this much information.

The Six Parts of a Telephone Script

A telephone script has six basic parts, as listed here:

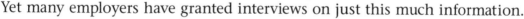

Part of Phone Script	What It Is
1. The target	The person who would supervise you
2. The name	Who you are

(continued)

(continued)

Part of Phone Script	What It Is
3. The job	What you want to do
4. The hook	What you have to offer
5. The goal	To get an interview or a referral
6. The closing	Saying thank you and goodbye

Here are more details on each part of a phone script:

1. **The target:** Do not ask for the personnel department. Instead, ask for the department where you would like to work. *May I please speak to the person in charge of the _____ department?*

2. **The name:** Give the employer your first and last name here, just like you would if you were introducing yourself in person. *Hello, my name is _____.*

3. **The job:** Give the job title or type of job you want here. *I am interested in a position as a _____.*

4. **The hook:** Include details from the Skills section of your JIST Card here.

   Example: *I'll be graduating in June from a two-year vocational program in _____, which included hands-on training. I've also taken _____ (one semester, one year, two years, and so on) of high school _____.*

   I have _____ (months/years) of _____ (various, other, or related) job experience. Some of my skills include _____ _____.

   (State three to five of your most impressive job-related or lab skills—tasks you already know how to do well.)

5. **The goal:** *When may I come in for an interview?*

✔ If you get an interview: Great. *I'm really interested in talking with you about this position. When would be a good time?* If you don't get an interview for a job that is open now, ask for an interview to discuss future openings and to learn more about the company.

✔ If you don't get an interview, ask all of the following: (a) *May I call you back about possible openings in the near future?* (b) *May I send you a resume?* and (c) *Do you know of anyone else I might contact?*

6. **The closing:** *Thank you very much for your time. I'll see you on* _____ _____ (date and time) *for my interview.*

> ❝*What lies behind us and what lies before us are tiny matters compared to what lies within us.*❞
>
> *Ralph Waldo Emerson*

ACTIVITY

Prepare Your Telephone Script

Each part of the phone script is covered in the following worksheet. Use the information from your JIST Card to fill out each section. Because people speak differently than they write, change the content of your JIST Card so that it sounds natural when spoken.

Before you complete the worksheet, use separate sheets of paper to create a rough draft of each worksheet section. Edit your material until it sounds good enough to write on the worksheet. You will write your complete, final telephone script at the end of this chapter.

TELEPHONE CONTACT WORKSHEET

1. **The target:** *May I please speak to the person in charge of the* _____ *department?*

2. **The name:** *Hello, my name is* _____.

3. **The job:** *I am interested in a position as a* _____.

4. **The hook:** Include details from the skills section of your JIST Card here.

    _____

    _____

    _____

    _____

5. **The goal:** *When may I come in for an interview?* If you are unable to get an interview, ask if you can call back and send a resume. Ask if the employer knows of any other organizations that would need someone with your skills.

6. **The closing:** *Thank you very much for your time. I'll see you on* _____ _____ (date and time) *for my interview.*

YOUR TURN

Make Your Phone Script Your Own

Keep rewriting your telephone script until it sounds right. The first five parts of the final version should take you between 25 and 30 seconds to read aloud in a conversational style. Rehearse it several times. Practice speaking distinctly, clearly, and with expression so that it sounds like normal conversation and not a written speech.

Reminders for Contacting Employers by Phone

✔ Get through to the hiring authority, the one person most likely to supervise you.

✔ Present your entire script. Do this clearly and without interruption.

✔ Get an interview. Be prepared to ask for an interview...

  * For the position you want. If no, then...

  * To discuss future openings. If no, then...

  * For information about the organization.

✔ If you do not get an interview:

  * Set up a date and time to call back.

  * Ask if you can send a resume.

  * Get a referral.

Overcome Typical Problems When Calling Employers

You now have a draft script to use in your phone calls. When you make your phone calls, you need to be prepared to handle several common problems. Here are some examples:

✔ How do you get past the operator, receptionist, or assistant who is trained to screen calls such as the one you are making?

✔ How do you get around voicemail to reach the person in charge?

✔ How do you respond to "Sorry, there are no openings"?

✔ How do you avoid an interview over the phone?

These are just a few of the situations that you may encounter as you make your telephone contacts. To overcome them, you need to have clear objectives and know a few helpful techniques.

Notice how the following common situations are handled. Do the tips help you meet the goals of a telephone contact?

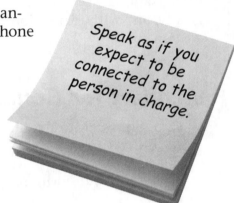

Speak as if you expect to be connected to the person in charge.

Situation 1: You ask to speak to the manager, supervisor, or director in charge of the job you are seeking. You do not want to get referred to the personnel department, told there are no openings, or get screened out by the receptionist. The receptionist wants to know why you are calling.

Prepare a response using the following tips:

✔ Sound businesslike and friendly. Speak as if you expect to talk to the right person. Begin by asking for the name of the person in charge of the area where you want to work. Then ask to be connected. In most cases, this will get you through.

✔ If you have been referred to the person you are calling, say that someone—a friend of the person you are calling—suggested that you call.

TIP

Try to get the name of the person in charge before you call. As mentioned in Chapter 6, many companies have Web sites that list contact names and phone numbers. Also, America's Career InfoNet at www.acinet.org gives key contact names and phone numbers for employers in every state.

✔ If you feel that you are being screened out, say that you want to send some material to the person, and you need the correct spelling of the name, title, and address. (This is true, because you will be sending a resume and JIST Card later.) Then call back tomorrow and ask for the person by name. Or call during lunch, when a replacement receptionist is likely to be on the phone.

TIP

If you get a voicemail message instead of an operator or receptionist, you can usually reach someone by pressing 0 or holding on the line. When a person answers, follow the previous points. If you get the voicemail of the person in charge, try calling back later.

Situation 2: The supervisor tells you there are no openings at the present time.

Prepare a response using the following tips:

✔ Don't give up! Show that you are still interested, and again ask for an interview. An employer will often consider a second request.

✔ Say that although no openings exist at present, you are still interested and would like to come in anyway to discuss future openings and to talk about the company.

✔ If you can't get an interview, ask if it is okay to send a resume and stay in touch. If so, ask if you can call back in about two weeks. Also ask for the names of other organizations that might need someone with your skills.

Situation 3: Because of your good presentation, the employer shows an interest in you and begins to ask you questions over the phone.

Prepare a response using the following tips:

✔ Ask if you can schedule an interview to cover in person any questions the employer might have. If that doesn't work, then...

✔ Tell the employer more about your special skills, experience, and training that qualify you for the job. Also do the following:

  ✱ Explain why you would be a good employee for this company.

  ✱ Ask questions about the company's service or products. Do not ask about pay or benefits.

  ✱ Close with a request for an interview.

TIP

Remember: Your main goal is to get an interview.

Contact Employers Using E-mail

Many employers prefer to be contacted via e-mail first. The reason is that e-mails don't interrupt their work day at inconvenient times. Following are tips for using e-mail to contact employers. Additional tips are included in the resume and other chapters later in this book.

- ✔ **Send e-mail to a specific person:** Get the name and e-mail address of the person most likely to hire or supervise you. You can often get this from the organization's Web site, sending an e-mail to the Web master asking for the contact information, or calling up and asking for it.

- ✔ **Try to be referred by someone else:** It is always best if you have been referred by someone the employer knows. Whenever this is the case, mention this in your e-mail subject line or early in your phone call or correspondence.

- ✔ **Keep your initial contact short and friendly:** Your initial objective is to get the employer to read and respond to your e-mail. Have a clear subject line so the employer knows it is not junk mail. Then include a few sentences telling the employer why you are contacting him or her and asking him or her to help you in your search for a job.

- ✔ **Ask for a response:** Depending on the situation, you can ask to come in to talk to the employer and ask for a time that would work for him or her. Alternatively, you could ask the employer to send you names of others to contact or to forward your e-mail to others.

- ✔ **Think carefully about using an attachment:** Many employers don't like e-mail attachments from people they don't know, because an attachment can contain a virus. Consider putting the text from your JIST Card at the end of the e-mail itself, or insert it as a graphics image. You can include a copy of your resume as an attachment in a later e-mail.

- ✔ **Check for good grammar and spelling before you send it:** Although e-mail is less formal than a letter, remember that your e-mail will make an impression. Make sure it is a good one!

- ✔ **Follow up:** After you get a response, follow up with additional information. Attach a copy of your resume, ask for a time to come in and talk with the employer, or ask this person to give you leads to other people who might be able to help you in your job search.

You can adopt many of the phone and other techniques you learn in this book for use with e-mail. More e-mail techniques are covered in other chapters. Be creative, and use e-mail along with other techniques to help you network and get interviews.

Contact Employers in Person

You can use your telephone script when making a personal visit to a place of business. Make sure you know your script well and have rehearsed it.

Stopping by a place of business or an organization without an appointment is okay. Some employers will be willing to see you on a short notice. Remember to dress professionally, as you would for an interview.

Goals for Contacting Employers in Person

✔ Ask to speak to the one person most likely to supervise you. This person also most likely would have the authority to hire you.

✔ Present your entire telephone script. Do this clearly and without interruption.

✔ Get an interview! Remember that your goal is to get an interview, so make sure you ask for one.

Ask for an interview...

✔ For the position you want. If no, then...

✔ To discuss future openings. If no, then...

✔ For information about the organization.

Chapter 11 explains what to do when you get a job interview. If the employer instead agrees either to discuss future openings or the organization (otherwise known as an *informational interview*), try to find out as much as you can about what the employer is looking for in an employee. Demonstrate your knowledge of the organization and the industry by asking questions about recent changes and future plans. You may be able to convince the employer at this point that you have the skills that the company needs. If not, ask for advice about how to be successful in this field. Listen closely and ask relevant questions. Taking notes will help you remember the most useful information. Before you leave, make sure you ask for a referral. Finally, don't forget to follow up with a note thanking the employer for meeting with you.

If You Do Not Get an Interview

For employers who can't see you, the visit can still be worthwhile if you do the following:

✔ Ask to make an appointment for another day and time.

✔ Leave your JIST Card and resume with the receptionist or supervisor's assistant. Ask that these documents be passed on to the supervisor.

✔ Ask for referrals to other companies that may be able to use your skills.

YOUR TURN

Create Your Final Script

Write out a final script based on your JIST Card. Write it just as you will say it on the phone and in person.

Practice your script and replies by yourself and with others until you feel comfortable and can say your script smoothly.

"Go confidently in the direction of your dreams. Live the life you have imagined."

Henry David Thoreau

Chapter 8

Write Great Cover Letters

Although phoning and dropping in on potential employers are effective job search methods, you will also need to contact employers in writing. Writing may be your only option for reaching some employers. Examples of when this may happen include the following:

✔ When ads require written or e-mail responses

✔ When you are not able to make personal contact with an employer, such as when the employer is rarely available, is on vacation, or is in the office during hours you are at school

✔ When the employer tells you to mail or e-mail a cover letter and resume

✔ When someone in your network tells you to write or e-mail an employer who may be interested in you

This written communication may be in the following formats:

✔ By a letter sent through the mail or dropped off at the employer's

✔ By fax

✔ By e-mail

In most instances, you should include your JIST Card and resume with any correspondence. Resumes are discussed in the next chapter.

What Is a Cover Letter?

Often referred to as a *cover letter* or *letter of application*, this correspondence will highlight much of the information you wrote in your telephone script. It should be brief, businesslike, and addressed to a specific person whenever possible. A cover letter should always accompany your resume.

How to Create Great Cover Letters

Without a strong cover letter, your wonderful resume may not get a first glance. The goals of the cover letter are as follows:

✔ Get potential employers interested in you.

✔ Impress them with your experience and skills related to a job opening.

✔ Show your interest in their company and their customers.

✔ Show that you are dependable, professional, and determined.

✔ Make employers want to look at your resume.

The cover letter is as important as your resume. Sample cover letters in this chapter show how to highlight experiences that will interest employers. Do not be bashful about saying that you were a champion swimmer, had a lead role in the school play, or are on the school's baseball team. Potential employers will think you are a great student with energy and enthusiasm. They will want you to bring that enthusiasm to their business. Let your cover letter highlight your strong points.

Let your cover letter highlight your strong points.

Tips to Make Your Cover Letter Look Good

To create a professional look, follow these tips:

✔ Give your cover letter the same look as your resume.

✔ Use the same type fonts and paper stock.

The material and examples on pages 98–105 are based on content from Creating Your High School Resume: A Step-by-Step Guide to Preparing an Effective Resume for College and Career *by Kathryn Kraemer Troutman. This workbook guides students through the process of creating their first cover letters and resumes. It is published by JIST Publishing, Inc.*

✔ Do not staple the letter and resume together because employers may want to photocopy your resume.

✔ Send the letter and resume in a matching envelope.

✔ If you're mailing to a large company, send the resume and letter flat in a large envelope in case your resume will be scanned.

Although you typically mail a cover letter with a resume, you can adapt many of the tips presented here for use with e-mail.

What Is Scanning?

Scanning is a technology that allows resumes to be "read" by Optical Character Readers (OCRs). The resume information is then saved in a computer database and searched by managers looking for employees with certain skills. Large companies use scanning to quickly find the most qualified applicants. Scanning is another important reason to use skill-related words in your resume and cover letter. Resumes that will be scanned should be formatted simply—sans serif type, no italic, no bullets, and no underlining. This will allow them to be scanned accurately.

Steps to Writing a Cover Letter

Using the following job ad from the *Washington Post,* you now will learn how to write a cover letter. We also use other examples here as needed. Here's the *Washington Post* ad:

TELEMARKETER. Enjoys speaking with the public. Articulate, computer literate with sales ability. 40 hours, 12 weeks. Send resume to Mr. Paul Jones, Supervisor, Smythe Corp., 1900 M St., NW, Wash., DC 20006. No calls accepted.

Step 1: Provide Your Contact Information

Start your cover letter with your contact information. Use the same format and type fonts as on your resume.

Kimberly Ann Garrett
2989 Smithwood Avenue
Annapolis, MD 99999
(555) 555-5555
E-mail: kimag@wishingwell.com

Step 2: State the Date

Next list the date, as you would on any business letter.

May 10, 20XX

Step 3: Enter the Contact Person's Name, Title, Employer, and Address

Then enter the contact person's name, title, employer, and mailing address. You need to have your letter on a computer so that you can personalize and modify it each time. Here is how to set up the person's name and address:

Mr. Paul Jones
Supervisor
Smythe Corp.
1900 M Street, NW
Washington, DC 20006

But what if you are applying for an advertised job that does not give an individual's name? Then try to find the name of the hiring person or the person reviewing incoming resumes. Put some effort into this research.

TIP Using a name can get your letter and resume to the hiring manager more quickly and can be an effective personal touch.

If you know which department has the opening, you can call the employer and ask the operator for the department manager's name. You can also search the employer's Web site and try to find the manager's name. If you're applying to a giant corporation and the ad says "Human Resources Director, Marriott Corporation," expect your resume to be scanned. You may not be able to get an individual's name.

Step 4: Include a Salutation

Here are your choices for addressing the contact person:

Dear Mr. Jones:	If a man's name is the contact
Dear Ms. Smith:	If a woman's name is the contact
Dear Prospective Employer:	If there is no name or if you're unsure of the person's gender

Step 5: Write the Opening Paragraph

Here are five types of opening paragraphs, depending on how you learned of the position.

Classified Advertisement

I read your advertisement in the May 10, 20XX, Washington Post *newspaper for a telemarketer position.*

Unsolicited Mailing

With an unsolicited mailing, you send your resume without being asked or without seeing a specific ad, just in case the employer needs someone like you. Unsolicited resumes are usually not very effective, so try to talk with managers at organizations that interest you before sending resumes.

I would like to apply for a position as telemarketer with Smythe Corporation. I am seeking a summer position where I can use my communications skills and work with the public.

The Internet

You may find job leads on Internet job databases and company Web sites. Here is how to write an opening paragraph for such a lead:

I am sending my attached resume as an application for the telemarketer position with your company. I found the opening listed on your Web site. Based on the description of Smythe Corporation, I would like to work for a company like yours. I am seeking a position where I can use my communications skills and work with the public.

Referral

A *referral* is a job lead from a neighbor, friend, mentor, or someone else in your network. Sometimes a person in your network will speak to the hiring person about you. As you learned earlier, this is often the best way to find a job. Employers appreciate referrals. Referrals save employers from reviewing hundreds of applications. Employers trust the recommendation of a valued employee or friend who stated that you would be a good employee. Sometimes departments are filled with the friends of a few people.

Referrals are the best way to get a job!

Here are three sample opening paragraphs for a cover letter based on a referral:

Sample 1: *I am sending my resume to you because of a referral from Mike Thomas, an associate in your Annapolis store. I am seeking a summer internship where I can use my communications skills and work with the public.*

Sample 2: *I was referred to you by Mike Thomas, who is my neighbor. He tells me that you frequently hire dependable, hard-working high school seniors in your department. Because you spend a great amount of time in the field, Mike recommended that I contact you in writing.*

Sample 3: *I was referred to you by Mike Thomas, who is a member of my church and a longtime family friend. I understand that you are hiring student interns in your customer service department. Mike recommended that I write to you and send my resume for your consideration.*

Previous Contact

If an employer you've contacted by phone asks you to send a resume, let your cover letter's opening paragraph remind the employer of your conversation. Don't just send a resume without a cover letter.

I am following up on the conversation we had today by phone. As requested, I am enclosing my resume, which provides more details on my skills and experience.

Step 6: Write the Middle Paragraph

Next is a summary of your background and critical skills to show that you are a match for the position:

> *As my resume shows, I am active in high school theater and had excellent roles in two plays. I am also successful in debate and student government. With these experiences, I can offer you excellent communication and interpersonal skills. I maintain a 3.0 average and work 10 hours per week during the school year. Familiarity with PCs, Windows, Word, and Excel is another skill I can bring to your department. I use the Internet regularly and can type more than 45 words per minute.*

Step 7: Write the Second Middle Paragraph

This is your persuasive paragraph with a few good-worker traits.

> *If you are seeking a dependable, hard-working, and friendly young person to work in your department for the summer, I would like to be considered.*

Step 8: Give Your Contact Information and Closing

> *I am available afternoons at (555) 555-5555 after 4 p.m. I have voicemail on that number. You can also reach me via e-mail at kimag@wishingwell.com. I will call you in a couple of days to see if I can make an appointment to discuss a summer position. Thank you for your time and consideration.*
>
> *Sincerely,*
>
> *Kimberly Ann Garrett*
>
> *Kimberly Ann Garrett*
>
> *Enclosure: resume*

If you are sending your resume and letter in response to a classified ad with no phone number or e-mail address, or if the company is large and receives hundreds of resumes, you may not be able to call. In that case, state "I look forward to hearing from you soon."

Think About the Employer's Needs

Think about the employer's products and services when you write your cover letter. Think about the hiring person's needs. How could you help this person with his or her department? Would you be good with the employer's customers? If so, the employer would be lucky to have you, right? Get the manager to recognize your interest and talents through your letter and resume.

Cover Letter Examples

The following student is responding to an ad for a part-time position in computer repair. The letter highlights his computer skills and experience. The bullet style is easy to read and write because each entry is a statement, not a full sentence. The paragraph style is written with full sentences. Which one do you prefer?

Here is the ad, followed by the student's letter:

Help Wanted: Computer Technician. Hardware and software experience. Must have Windows conversion experience. Ability to communicate with non-technical users. One year of experience required. 20 hours/week. Send resume and letter only. Andy E. Quinn, ABC Computers, 322 Smith St., Lockport, NY 20000. No phone calls.

Garth Torres
618 Willingham Road
Little Valley, New York 20000
(555) 555-3333
E-mail: gtorres@com.com

September 18, 20XX

Mr. Andy E. Quinn
ABC Computers
322 Smith Street
Lockport, New York 20000

Dear Mr. Quinn:

I am responding to your advertisement in the *Lockport Gazette* for a computer technician in your computer repair business.

Block paragraph style

As a senior at Little Valley Central High School in Little Valley, New York, I have completed numerous computer courses, including Microsoft Suite and PCs. I have upgraded the hardware and software of my own PC over the past three years. I successfully upgraded my system and friends' PCs to the newest version of Windows. As an assistant in the school's computer lab, I help students with various student computer needs. I am a student support person for the office as well.

I can offer your computer firm the following qualifications:

Bullet style

- Senior at Little Valley Central High School, Little Valley, New York, with 20 hours per week available.
- Completed five courses in computers, including Microsoft Suite, PC Maintenance, and the Windows Operating System.
- Owned and operated PCs for three years.
- Installed software, including operating systems and applications programs; upgraded memory and hardware.
- Assistant in computer lab and school office for eight months; help with 15 PCs.

You will find me to be hard working, energetic, and able to work without supervision. I also communicate well with users and coworkers.

I would like to work part-time throughout my senior year in high school to gain more hands-on experience in computer repair, troubleshooting, and installation. I am available for an interview at your convenience.

Sincerely,

Garth Torres

Garth Torres

Enclosure: Resume

Your address and current date

337 North Main Street
Anytown, Pennsylvania 00001
January 10, 20XX

Mr. James Stone
General Manager
Continental Corporation
328 Fifth Avenue
Anytown, Pennsylvania 00001

Name of person and company you are applying to

Dear Mr. Stone:

Mention when you are available for employment

Mention how you learned of the position

I understand from my vocational instructor, Mr. William Jones, that there is now an opening in your department.

As a senior at the County Joint Vocational School in Anytown, Pennsylvania, I will be available for early work placement at the end of January. My previous experience and educational background are outlined in the enclosed resume. I hope you will agree that my background in criminal justice would be an asset to your department. I will be graduating this coming June and expect to receive both my vocational certificate and my high school diploma.

In addition to my experience, I possess skills in organization and communication. I am also reliable and hard working.

May I talk with you about this opening? I will arrange to come for an interview at your convenience. My home telephone number is (555) 555-0000. I look forward to your reply.

Request an interview

Sincerely,

Jennifer R. York

Jennifer R. York

Summarize your background and skills to show that you are a match for the job

Sign your name neatly in blue or black ink

Enclosure

ACTIVITY

Write a Cover Letter

This worksheet will help you draft a cover letter that you can use in many situations. You can easily modify it to fit the job, employer, and skills needed.

COVER LETTER WORKSHEET

Your street address:_____

Your city, state, ZIP code, e-mail address:_____

_____

Today's date:_____

Contact person's full name (including Mr. or Ms.):_____

Contact person's title:_____

Contact person's place of employment:_____

Contact person's street address:_____

Contact person's city, state, ZIP code, e-mail address:_____

_____

Dear Mr./Ms:_____

Opening paragraph: Write a brief statement of why you are sending this letter.

_____

_____

_____

_____

_____

(continued)

(continued)

Middle paragraph: Compose a few sentences that would persuade an employer to hire you. Highlight some of your skills and how they would relate to the job.

_____

_____

_____

_____

_____

Second middle paragraph: This is your persuasive paragraph that mentions a few good-worker traits. _____

_____

_____

_____

_____

Final paragraph: Request an interview and include how and when you can be reached. If you know how to reach the employer, mention when you will call as a follow-up. _____

_____

_____

_____

_____

Sincerely,

Your signature:_____

Your name typed:_____

Enclosure(s)

Points to Consider When Sending Faxes

An employer may request that you fax your resume. If so, make sure that you include your cover letter so that it gets to the right person. It is better, however, to mail the documents or drop them off in person. Your originals will make a stronger impression. You only get one chance to create a first impression, so you want it to be your best.

Another option is to fax your cover letter and resume and then follow up with copies in the mail.

Points to Consider When Sending E-mail

Although e-mail has made it faster and easier to transmit information you will lose the quality look of your cover letter and resume. Remember that a first impression may be the only chance you get. Make sure you put your best foot forward.

Many employers fear viruses hidden in attached files. So if an ad or an employer asks you to send your material by e-mail, copy and paste the text into the body of an e-mail rather than attaching it as a separate file. You will need to adjust the look of the text in the e-mail so that everything lines up correctly. Then follow up by sending your cover letter and resume in the mail. More details on electronic resumes will be provided in another chapter.

YOUR TURN

Create Your Own Cover Letter

Create a draft copy of your cover letter. Edit and proofread your letter so that it is error free. Check for spelling, grammar, and typographical errors. Don't trust spell checkers alone!

"Who has confidence in himself will gain the confidence of others."

Leib Lazarow

Chapter 9

Write an Effective Resume

You have learned that sending out resumes at random is not an effective job-seeking technique. Many employers, however, will ask you for a resume because resumes are a useful tool to help them screen people.

A well-done resume will tell an employer who you are and how to contact you. It will give a brief review of your background, work, education, life experience, skills, and abilities in a more detailed manner than the information found on your JIST Card.

The Chronological Resume

Although other resume formats exist, most people use a *chronological resume,* which is a simple resume that presents your experience in reverse chronological order. The most recent experience is listed first, followed by previous experience. As a high school student, you can include sections on your extracurricular activities, achievements, awards, volunteer experiences, and skills.

Resume Examples

Look over the following examples of vocational and high school students' resumes. Use them as your guide for completing the Resume Worksheet at the end of this chapter.

66*Integrity ... is your inner image of yourself,
and if you look in there and see someone who
won't cheat, then you know he never will.*99

John D. MacDonald

73990 Smith Valley Road   Phone (555) 999-9999
Medford, California 44444   E-mail shall@netcom.net

Scott Hall

Objective	To attend a four-year college and receive a degree in business.

Education

West Hill High School   1000 Main Street
Received Diploma June 20XX   Medford, California 44444
                                 (555) 999-0000

Awards Received

- **3.8 GPA**
- **Honor Roll (4 years)**
- **Listed in Who's Who Among American High School Students**
- **Americanism and Government Test Winner (2 years)**
- **Northern Conference Scholar Athlete (2 years)**

Work Experience

Summers of 20XX and 20XX   *20XX-20XX*

Ken Jones   City Auto Parts, Inc.
390 Beloit Road   6666 Smith Avenue
Medford, California 44444   Medford, California 44444
(555) 555-9999   (555) 888-4444
Loaded/unloaded wagons;   Sorted parts; stocked shelves;
  baled hay   recorded inventory

Volunteer Experience

- Church Youth Group (5 years)
- Northern Canada Missionary Programs (3 years)

Extracurricular Activities

- Future Problem Solving, state champions (4 years)
- Debate (2 years)
- Student Council (2 years)
- Students Against Drunk Driving (3 years)
- Drama, various productions (3 years)

Roberta B. Hired

37 Main Street   **Boise, Idaho 00000**   **(555) 666-7777**   **rhired@connect.com**

OBJECTIVE   To secure a position in the field of Health Technologies or related work.

EDUCATION

September 20XX-   Lake County JVS   Degree: Vocational Certificate
June 20XX   Boise, Idaho   Major: Health Technology Tech Prep

September 20XX-   Neighborhood High School   Degree: High School Diploma
June 20XX   Boise, Idaho   Major: College Prep/Academic

EXPERIENCE

April 20XX-   Ashley Place Health Care   Position: Nursing Assistant
Present   Boise, Idaho   Duties: Provide quality nursing care to
                                                 residents.

March 20XX-   Taco Bell   Position: Crew Member
October 20XX   Boise, Idaho   Duties: Took and filled customer orders,
                                                 prepared food items, handled money, and
                                                 maintained sanitary conditions.

May 20XX-   Self-Employed   Position: Babysitter
September 20XX   Boise, Idaho   Duties: Supervised the safety and
                                                 activities of children for six families.

ACHIEVEMENTS   Eligible for Emergency Medical Technician (EMT) National Registry Certification
                       Eligible for American Society of Phlebotomy Technologists (ASPT) Certification
                       Health Care Provider CPR Certification from the American Heart Association
                       Honor Roll student – Freshman through senior years
                       Inducted into the National Honor Society – Junior year

ACTIVITIES   Vocational Industrial Clubs of America – Two years
                       Marching Band – Four years
                       Mentoring experience at Boardman X-Ray

SKILLS
- Medical Terminology
- Anatomy/Physiology
- Computer Literacy
- Phlebotomy
- Emergency Medical Technology

PERSONAL   I take pride in my work, follow directions well, and am willing to learn new skills.
                       I am dependable, honest, and very hard working. I have an excellent attendance record.

James Cook

5584 Boardman Road   **St. Louis, Missouri 66688**   **(333) 555-0000**

Objective
To obtain summer employment.

Education
ST. LOUIS HIGH SCHOOL   ST. LOUIS, MISSOURI
Degree: High School Honors Diploma, June 20XX
Major: Academic/College Prep
Rank: Top 15%, 61st of 424 students
National Honor Society, two years
Varsity Football Team, three years, lettered twice
Junior Varsity Football Team, two years
Sophomore Football Team, one year
Freshman Football Team, one year, lettered
Varsity Swim Team, one year, lettered

Volunteer Work
State of Missouri Senior Olympics – set up swim meet; head timer
St. Louis Area Special Olympics – set up swim meet; head timer
St. Louis YMCA – head operator of timing console for home swim meets

Experience
ST. LOUIS COUNTRY CLUB   ST. LOUIS, MISSOURI
Head Golf Caddie   **Summers of 20XX and 20XX**
Duties included instructing caddies in the proper procedures and
etiquette of golf and caddying for club members.

Awards
Inducted into the National Honor Society
Received two varsity letters in football
Received one varsity letter in swimming
Placed first in the 20XX YCC Pentathlon Swim Meet

Personal
Extremely hard working and dedicated to whatever I am assigned or
attempt to do on my own. Constantly striving to improve and to perform
to the best of my ability.

Krista J. Johnson

317 Wright Avenue   Nashua, New Hampshire 88888
Home Phone (333) 444-4444   Email kjohnson@connect.net

Objective
To obtain a Bachelor of Music Degree in Vocal Performance and Education at a four-year college and also a Master's Degree in Vocal Performance Pedagogy to become a professional singer and voice instructor.

Education
East Fork High School, Nashua, New Hampshire
Graduation expected June 20XX

Work Experience
September 20XX-current
Jane's Boutique
2500 West Main Street
Nashua, New Hampshire
(333) 444-8899
Sales Associate

Extracurricular Activities
- Choir (3 years)
- Musicals (leading roles, 3 years)
- Drama (2 years)
- PA Crew (2 years)
- Future Teachers of America (board of directors, 1 year)

Achievements
- Superior Ratings in State Vocal Music Contests (3 years)
- Mount Union College Junior Scholar (2 years)

Volunteer Experience
- Assistant to Vocal Music Teacher (3 years)
- Sang in Area Nursing Homes (2 years)
- Taught Bible School at my church (1 year)

Pat J. Gordon

327 Main Street   Atlanta, Georgia 22222
Home (999) 888-8888   Cell Phone (999) 666-6666

Objective   To secure a position in the field of building, remodeling, and
maintenance.

Education

September 20XX-   Local County JVS   Degree: Vocational Certificate
June 20XX   Atlanta, Georgia   Major: Building, Remodeling,
                                      and Maintenance

September 20XX-   Local High School   Degree: High School Diploma
June 20XX   Atlanta, Georgia   Major: College Prep/Business

Experience

April 20XX-   Gates Custom Homes   Position: Carpenter's Assistant
Present   Dunwoody, Georgia   Duties: Lay out cuts, nail
                                       patterns, clean up work area.

March 20XX-   Atlanta Beacon   Position: Paper Carrier
October 20XX   Atlanta, Georgia   Duties: Delivered daily
                                       newspapers to 50 customers;
                                       collected monthly payments;
                                       kept accurate records.

May 20XX-   Self-Employed   Position: Lawn Care
September 20XX   Duties: Mowed and trimmed
                                       yards for six families; pruned
                                       bushes; weeded flower beds.

Achievements   Placed first in regional VICA Carpentry Event, junior year
Perfect Attendance Award, senior year
Certificate of Achievement in Building and Remodeling

Activities   Vocational Industrial Clubs of America, two years
Senior Building, Remodeling, and Maintenance Class
President

Skills   Carpentry: framing, decks, roofs, trim, and cabinetry
Drywall: hanging, finishing, repairing, and texturing
Wiring: residential and EMT
Plumbing: basic and residential
Siding: vinyl, vertical, and wood
Roofing: shingle, gutter, flashing, and drip edge
Masonry: brick, block, and pointing
Blueprints: draw and read

Professional, Trustworthy, Dependable, Motivated

Describing Your Jobs on Your Resume

Following are commonly held jobs and their required duties. This information may help you complete the Resume Worksheet.

Field	Position	Duties
Fast foods	Crew member	Take and fill customer orders, operate cash register, and maintain sanitary conditions. (OR) Expedite customer orders at counter and at drive-thru, handle money, and maintain clean and orderly work area.
Babysitting	Babysitter for the Robert Smith family	Supervise the safety and activities of three young children, prepare snacks and meals, and do light housecleaning.
Paper boy	Paper carrier	Deliver daily newspapers to 50 customers, collect monthly payments, and maintain accurate records.
Medical occupation	Dietary aid	Prepare trays for residents according to specific dietary needs; sanitize dishes, glassware, utensils, pots, and pans; and keep work area clean and orderly.
Child care	Prekindergarten teacher	Oversee the safety and play of young children and the feeding and changing of infants.
Grocery store	Customer service	Bag grocery items, assist customers in loading their vehicles, stock and face shelves and displays, and maintain clean and orderly conditions.

(continued)

(continued)

Field	Position	Duties
Grocery store	Cashier	Ring up customer sales using proper store codes; process cash, check, food stamps, and credit card payments; bag items; and maintain clean work area.
Lifeguard	Lifeguard	Supervise the safety and activities of patrons, perform CPR and administer first aid when needed, and enforce pool rules.
Gas station	Fuel attendant	Pump gas; wash windows; check fluids; service tires; and process cash, check, and credit card payments.
Landscaping	Landscaper	Seed, sod, mow, weed, fertilize, water, and aerate customer lawns; plant and transplant shrubs, trees, and flowers; build rock walls; and install fountains.
Lawn care	Lawn care	Maintain yards for 10 customers; mow, trim, and edge lawns; prune hedges and shrubs; and weed and mulch beds.
Restaurant	Bus person	Clear, clean, and set tables; assist servers as needed; and maintain sanitary conditions.
Movie theater	Cashier/usher	Sell and collect movie tickets, expedite snack orders, handle money, stock supplies and food items, direct customers to proper theater areas, and maintain clean conditions.
Fair parking	Parking attendant	Direct fair traffic to designated parking areas.

ACTIVITY

Begin Your Resume

Use the worksheet that follows to organize your personal information. Review Chapters 3 through 5 and the *Data Minder* for the skills and other details to use in your worksheet. Also, you can refer to the sample resumes and the earlier section titled "Describing Your Jobs on Your Resume."

Make sure you complete the Resume Worksheet carefully by printing neatly in pencil and avoiding abbreviations. Later, you can use the information from this worksheet to create your chronological resume.

THE RESUME WORKSHEET

Full name: _____

Address: _____

City, state, ZIP code: _____

Area code and phone number: _____

Area code and alternative phone number: _____

E-mail address: _____

Objective

To secure a position in _____

_____

_____

_____

(continued)

(continued)

Education

Name of high school: _____

Degree: _____

City, state: _____

Major: _____

Name of high school: _____

Degree: _____

City, state: _____

Major: _____

Experience (Most recent job first. Include both paid and unpaid work.)

Company name: _____

Position: _____

City, state: _____

Duties include: _____

_____

Company name: _____

Position: _____

City, state: _____

Duties include: _____

_____

Company name: _____

Position: _____

City, state: _____

Duties include:_____

_____

Achievements (Include awards, ribbons, trophies, certificates.)

_____

_____

_____

_____

Activities (Groups, clubs, teams, music. Include number of years of membership or participation.)

_____

_____

_____

_____

Skills

_____

_____

_____

_____

Personal (Compose three sentences describing your good-worker traits.)

_____

_____

_____

_____

Tips for Preparing a Superior Resume

The following tips can help you create a superior resume:

✔ **Write it yourself:** It's okay to look at other resumes for ideas, but write yours yourself. It will force you to organize your thoughts and background.

✔ **Make it error free:** One spelling or grammar error will create a negative impression. Get someone else to review your final draft for errors. Then review it again!

✔ **Make it look good:** Poor copy quality, cheap paper, bad type quality, or anything that creates a sloppy physical appearance will turn off employers.

✔ **Be brief and be relevant:** Many good resumes fit on one page. Few justify more than two. Include only the most important points. Use short sentences and action words. If it doesn't relate to and support your job objective, take it out!

✔ **Be honest:** Don't overstate your qualifications. If you end up getting a job you can't handle, it will not be to your advantage.

✔ **Be positive:** Emphasize your accomplishments and results. This is no place to be too humble or to display your faults.

✔ **Be specific:** Rather than saying "I am good with people," say "I supervised four people in the warehouse and increased productivity by 30%." Use numbers whenever possible (people served, percentage increased, dollar increased, and so on).

✔ **Edit:** Write each of your resume drafts on a separate piece of paper. Make every word count. Keep editing until your resume is as good as you can make it. Then edit it again.

✔ **Use action words and short sentences:** Look at the sample resumes for ideas.

✔ **Avoid anything negative:** If an employer might consider something on your resume as negative, cut it.

Tips for Producing Your Resume

Producing a resume can be confusing. The following tips can help you produce one that will make you proud:

✔ **Review your resume:** Have someone else review the final draft. Pick someone who will find spelling, grammar, and other errors. A teacher or counselor is a good choice.

✔ **Resume formatting:** Use a basic word processing program to create your resume. Many word processing programs have resume templates or step-by-step guidance to help you design your resume. If you don't have a home computer, use one at school or the library.

TIP Be sure to save your resume on your computer for easy updating later.

✔ **Quality printing:** Output your final resume on a laser printer. Make sure you will be able to produce extra copies as needed.

✔ **Paper:** Use good-quality paper. If you prefer a color, use ivory, cream, light gray, or any other soft color that you can find in an office supply store.

✔ **Other alternatives:** Take your resume on disk to a local printer and have it printed professionally. Many quick-copy stores provide this service for a small fee.

Electronic and Scannable Resumes

If you plan to use the Internet in your job search, you will need to submit your resume in electronic format. That way, employers can enter your resume into a database and search for keywords.

Even if you don't plan to use the Internet, you need to understand how electronic resumes work. More and more employers are scanning the resumes they receive.

Scanners are machines that convert your resume into electronic text. This allows employers to use a computer to quickly search hundreds or thousands of resumes to find qualified applicants. The computers look for keywords in the resumes—usually qualifications and skills that match the criteria needed for the open positions—and sort out the resumes with the most "hits."

Many larger employers use scanning technology. They're likely to scan your paper resume into a database without your knowing it. Because electronic resumes are used differently than those on paper, it is important to understand how you can increase their effectiveness and their "readability" by a machine.

An Electronic Resume Should Have Many Keywords

Employers who use electronic databases search for keywords in resumes. The more keywords you include, the more likely your resume will be selected. *Keywords* are words and phrases that are specific to the job you want. Here are some ways to find and present keywords on your resume:

✔ Add a keyword section.

A simple technique is to add a section to your resume titled "Key Skills." Then you can add keywords that aren't included elsewhere in your resume.

✔ Include all your important skill words.

If you completed the worksheets in steps 1 and 2, include the key skills documented there.

✔ Think like a prospective employer.

List the jobs you want. Then think of the keywords that employers are likely to use when searching a database.

✔ Review job descriptions.

Carefully review descriptions for jobs you seek in major print references like the *Occupational Outlook Handbook* and the *O*NET Dictionary of Occupational Titles*. Most large Web sites that list job openings have lots of employer job postings and job descriptions to review. Corporate Web sites often post information on job openings, which is another source of keywords. Make a list of keywords in descriptions of interest, and include them in your resume.

A resume is not the most effective tool for getting interviews.

✔ Be specific.

List certifications and licenses, name any software and machines you can operate, and include special language and abbreviations used in your field.

A better approach is to make direct contact with those who hire or supervise people with your skills and ask them for an interview, even if no openings exist now. *Then* send a resume.

For an Electronic Resume, a Simple Design Is Best

The databases that your resume goes into want only text, not design. Scanners introduce fewer errors when the text is simple. What this means is that you need to take out your resume's carefully done format and design elements and reduce your resume to the simplest text format. Follow these guidelines:

✔ No graphics

✔ No lines

✔ No bold, italic, or other text variations

✔ Only one easy-to-scan font

✔ No tab indentations

✔ No line or paragraph indents

✔ No centering; align text to the left

This may be discouraging, but it's the way electronic resumes work most effectively.

Tips to Convert Your Paper Resume to an Electronic One

Fortunately, you can easily take your existing resume and reformat it for electronic submission. Here are some quick tips for doing so:

✔ Cut and paste your resume text into a new file in your word processor.

✔ Eliminate any graphics elements, such as lines or images.

✔ Set your margins so that text is no more than 65 characters wide.

✔ Use one easy-to-scan font, such as Courier, Arial, Helvetica, or Times Roman. Eliminate bold, italic, and other font styles.

✔ Introduce major sections with words in all uppercase letters, rather than in bold or a different font.

A Few Final Words on Resumes

Before you write and use your resume, here is some advice that applies to both paper and electronic resumes:

✔ Even the best of resumes will not get you a job.

You have to do that yourself. To do so, you have to get interviews and do well in them. Interviews are where the job search action is, not resumes.

✔ Don't listen to resume experts.

If you ask 10 people for advice on your resume, all will be willing to give it—yet no 2 will agree. You have to make up your own mind about your resume. Feel free to break any "rules" if you have a good reason.

✔ **Don't avoid the job search by worrying about your resume.**

Write a simple and error-free resume, and then go out and get lots of interviews. Later, you can write a better resume—if you want or need to.

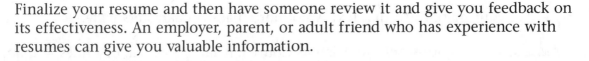

The Cover Letter

Always include a cover letter when sending your resume to an employer.

The cover letter should be brief, attract the employer's attention, and introduce you to the employer in a positive and professional way. Use the cover letter you developed in Chapter 8 as a guide. Remember to check the name, title, and address of employers that you are writing to.

YOUR TURN

Finalize Your Resume

Finalize your resume and then have someone review it and give you feedback on its effectiveness. An employer, parent, or adult friend who has experience with resumes can give you valuable information.

Chapter 10

Avoid the Application Trap

Many people think that filling out an application is the same as applying for a job. It isn't! Most employers use applications to screen people *out*, not in. If your application is messy, incomplete, or shows you do not have the right experience or training, you probably will not get an interview.

Although many smaller employers don't use applications, other employers will ask you to fill them out. For this reason, it is important to know how to complete applications properly.

ACTIVITY

Albert C. Smith's Less-Than-Perfect Application

Seeing someone else make mistakes on a job application can help you avoid the same mistakes. Meet Albert C. Smith. Like many of you, he wants to find a job. This activity shows you an application that Albert completed at a department store. It is reproduced on the next two pages.

I am sure you will agree that Albert could have done a better job of completing his application. Your job is to review Albert's application and circle the mistakes he made. There are more than 30 mistakes in this application. See how many you can find.

(continued)

(continued)

Date *April 1*

APPLICATION FOR EMPLOYMENT

PLEASE PRINT INFORMATION REQUESTED IN INK.

BROWN'S IS AN EQUAL OPPORTUNITY EMPLOYER and fully subscribes to the principles of Equal Employment Opportunity. Brown's has adopted an Affirmative Action Program to ensure that all applicants and employees are considered for hire, promotion and job status, without regard to race, color, religion, sex, national origin, age, handicap, or status as a disabled veteran or veteran of the Vietnam Era.

To protect the interests of all concerned, applicants for certain job assignments must pass a physical examination before they are hired.

Note: This application will be considered active for 90 days. If you have not been employed within this period and are still interested in employment at Brown's, please contact the office where you applied and request that your application be reactivated.

Name *Albert C. Smith*   Last / First / Middle   Social Security Number *411-¥76-2614* (Please present your Social Security Card for review)

Address *1526 N. Otter*   Number / Street / City / State / Zip Code

County *Marion*

Current phone or nearest phone _____

Previous Address *Same*   Number / Street / City / State / Zip Code

Best time of day to contact *any*
(Answer only if position for which you are applying requires driving)

If hired, can you furnish proof of age? ✓ Yes ___ No

Licensed to drive car? ___ Yes ___ No

If hired, can you furnish proof that you are legally entitled to work in U.S.? ✓ Yes ___ No

Is license valid in this state? ___ Yes ___ No

Have you ever been employed by Brown's. Yes ___ No X If so, when ___ X Position ___

Have you a relative in the employment of Brown's Department Store? Yes ___ No X

A PHYSICAL OR MENTAL DISABILITY WILL NOT CAUSE REJECTION IF IN BROWN'S MEDICAL OPINION YOU ARE ABLE TO SATISFACTORILY PERFORM IN THE POSITION FOR WHICH YOU ARE BEING CONSIDERED. Alternative placement, if available, of an applicant who does not meet the physical standards of the job for which he/she was originally considered is permitted.

Do you have any physical or mental impairment which may limit your ability to perform the job for which you are applying? *Yes I have a back problem & was in Central State Hospital for 6 months.*

If yes, what can reasonably be done to accommodate your limitation? _____

	School Attended	No. of Years	Name of School	City/State	Graduate?	Course or College Major	Average Grades
EDUCATION	Grammar	6	Holy Trinity	Scranton	Yes	General	B
	Jr. High	3	Crestview	"	"	"	B
	Sr. High	3	WCHS	"	"	College Prep	C
	Other			"	"		
	College	3	State U	Scranton	NO		C

	Branch of Service	Date Entered Service	Date of Discharge	Highest Rank Held	Service-Related Skills and Experience Applicable to Civilian Employment
MILITARY SERVICE	USA	1999	2003	E-3	¥ radio stuff

What experience or training have you had other than your work experience, military service and education? (Community activities, hobbies, etc.) _____

I am interested in the type of work I have checked:

Sales X   Office X   Mechanical ¥✓   Warehouse X   Other (Specify): ✓

Or the following specific job *anything*

I am seeking (check only one):

✓ Temporary employment (6 days or less)

✓ Seasonal employment (one season, e.g. Christmas)

✓ Regular employment (employment for indefinite period of time)

I am available for (check only one):

✓ Part-Time

✓ Full-Time

Work

If part-time, indicate maximum hours per week and enter hours available in block to the right.

If temporary, indicate dates available _____

Have you been convicted during the past seven years of a serious crime involving a person's life or property?

NO X   YES ¥   If yes, explain: *drunk in public*

HOURS AVAILABLE FOR WORK	
Sunday	To
Monday	To
Tuesday	To
Wednesday	To *anytime*
Thursday	To
Friday	To
Saturday	To

REFERENCES

LIST BELOW YOUR FOUR MOST RECENT EMPLOYERS, BEGINNING WITH THE CURRENT OR MOST RECENT ONE. IF YOU HAVE HAD FEWER THAN FOUR EMPLOYERS, USE THE REMAINING SPACES FOR PERSONAL REFERENCES. IF YOU WERE EMPLOYED UNDER A MAIDEN OR OTHER NAME, PLEASE ENTER THAT NAME IN THE RIGHT HAND MARGIN. IF APPLICABLE, ENTER SERVICE IN THE ARMED FORCES ON THE REVERSE SIDE.

NAMES AND ADDRESSES OF FORMER EMPLOYERS BEGINNING WITH THE CURRENT OR MOST RECENT	Nature of Employer's Business	What kind of work did you do?	Name of Your Supervisor	Starting Date	Starting Pay	Date of Leaving	Pay at Leaving	Why did you leave? Give details
Name: ABC — Tel. No. — Address: Walnut St. — Zip Code — City: Scranton — State: PA	School	Clean up	Eric Burgess	Month ? Year 04	$7 an hr.	Month 3 Year 05		Fired
NOTE: State reason for and length of inactivity between present application date and last employer. — looked for a job — almost a year								
Name: Fred Willis — Tel. No. — Address: ? — Zip Code — City: Scranton — State: PA	Houses	electrician helper labore	Rafael	Month 8 Year 05	$6.50 an hr	Month Year	$6.50	Boss always picked on me.
NOTE: State reason for and length of inactivity between present application date and last employer.								
Name: Wayne Const. — Tel. No. 555-4141 — Address: 143th N. Anderson — Zip Code — City: Scranton — State: PA	Construction	Jack hammer + wiring	Kimberwick	Month 6 Year 98	$6 an hr.	Month 4 Year 99	$6.25	Company went broke.
NOTE: State reason for and length of inactivity between present application date and last employer.								
Name: Central Hospital — Tel. No. — Address: Washington St. — Zip Code — City: Scranton — State: PA	Mental hospital	Clean up	Lynn Donovan	Month ? Year ?	$5.50 an hr	Month Year	same	I got better was discharged.
NOTE: State reason for and length of inactivity between present application date and last employer.								

I certify that the information in this application is correct to the best of my knowledge and understand that any misstatement or omission of information is grounds for dismissal in accordance with Brown's policy. I authorize the references listed above to give you any and all information concerning my previous employment and any pertinent information they may have, personal or otherwise, and release all parties from all liability for any damage that may result from furnishing same to you. In consideration of my employment, I agree to conform to the rules and regulations of Brown's, and my employment and compensation can be terminated with or without cause, and with or without notice, at any time, at the option of either the Company or myself. I understand that no unit manager or representative of Brown's other than the President or Vice-President of the company, has any authority to enter into any agreement for employment for any specified period of time, or to make any agreement contrary to the foregoing. In some states, the law requires that Brown's have my written permission before obtaining consumer reports on me, and I hereby authorize Brown's to obtain such reports.

Applicant's Signature _Smith, Albert C._

NOT TO BE FILLED OUT BY APPLICANT

Tested	(Store will enter dates as required.)
Physical examination scheduled for _blank_	REFERENCE REQUESTS
Physical examination form completed	CONSUMER REPORT
	With. Tax (W-4)
	State With. Tax

Date of Emp.	
Dept or Div.	Regular ___ Part-time ___
Job Title	Job Grade
Job Title Code	
Compensation Arrangement	Make me an offer
Manager Approving	
Employee No.	

		Mailed	Completed
REFERENCE REQUESTS		not yet	
CONSUMER REPORT			

Review Card prepared		Minor's Work Permit	
Timecard prepared		Proof of Birth	
		Training Material Given to Employee	

INTERVIEWER'S COMMENTS: I really need a job now.

I didn't get one.

Prospect for
1.
2.

Albert Smith

Unit Name and Number

Tips on Picking Up and Dropping Off Applications

The following tips will help you avoid problems and make a good impression as you apply for a job:

✔ Dress appropriately when you pick up, fill out, or drop off applications from employers.

✔ Do not bring anyone with you when applying for jobs or going on interviews.

✔ If possible, complete applications at home so you can fill them out with the greatest care.

✔ Be sure to proofread your applications to correct any errors.

✔ Try to meet employers to hand in applications directly and ask for interviews. If unable to do so, be sure to call each employer after a few days to make sure the employer received your application. Tell the employer that you are still interested in the position and then set up an interview. Remember: You can make only one first impression, so let it be positive.

✔ Allow extra time in your schedule when you return an application—just in case the employer asks you to stay for an interview.

ACTIVITY

Albert C. Smith's Improved Application

Albert C. Smith's application has many mistakes. How many did you find? It would not make a good impression on any employer. It is messy, includes negative information, and has many other problems.

The example on pages 131–132 shows what Albert C. Smith's application looks like when properly filled out.

Look it over and see how many errors you found in the original version that were corrected on the improved version.

APPLICATION FOR EMPLOYMENT

PLEASE PRINT INFORMATION REQUESTED IN INK.

Date **April 1, 20xx**

BROWN'S IS AN EQUAL OPPORTUNITY EMPLOYER and fully subscribes to the principles of Equal Employment Opportunity. Brown's has adopted an Affirmative Action Program to ensure that all applicants and employees are considered for hire, promotion and job status, without regard to race, color, religion, sex, national origin, age, handicap, or status as a disabled veteran or veteran of the Vietnam Era.

To protect the interests of all concerned, applicants for certain job assignments must pass a physical examination before they are hired.

Note: This application will be considered active for 90 days. If you have not been employed within this period and are still interested in employment at Brown's, please contact the office where you applied and request that your application be reactivated.

Name **Smith** (Last) **Albert** (First) **Claude** (Middle)   Social Security Number **411-76-2614**
(Please present your Social Security Card for review)

Address **1526** (Number) **North Otter Street** (Street) **Scranton** (City) **PA** (State) **18602** (Zip Code)

County _____

Previous Address _____ (Number) _____ (Street) _____ (City) _____ (State) _____ (Zip Code)

Current phone or nearest phone **555-1212**

Best time of day to contact **after 12 p.m.**

If hired, can you furnish proof of age? **✓** Yes _____ No

If hired, can you furnish proof that you are legally entitled to work in U.S. **✓** Yes _____ No

(Answer only if position for which you are applying requires driving)
Licensed to drive car? **✓** Yes _____ No
Is license valid in this state? **✓** Yes _____ No

Have you ever been employed by Brown's. Yes _____ No **✓** If so, when _____ Position _____

Have you a relative in the employment of Brown's Department Store? Yes _____ No **✓**

A PHYSICAL OR MENTAL DISABILITY WILL NOT CAUSE REJECTION IF IN BROWN'S MEDICAL OPINION YOU ARE ABLE TO SATISFACTORILY PERFORM IN THE POSITION FOR WHICH YOU ARE BEING CONSIDERED. Alternative placement, if available, of an applicant who does not meet the physical standards of the job for which he/she was originally considered is permitted.

Do you have any physical or mental impairment which may limit your ability to perform the job for which you are applying? **No** _____

If yes, what can reasonably be done to accommodate your limitation? _____

	School Attended	No. of Years	Name of School	City/State	Graduate?	Course or College Major	Average Grades
EDUCATION	Grammar	6	Holy Trinity	Scranton, PA		General	B
	Jr. High	3	Crestview Junior H.S.	Scranton, PA		General	B
	Sr. High	3	Warren Central H.S.	Scranton, PA		College Prep	C
	Other	—			—		
	College	3	Indiana – Purdue University at Indpls	Indpls, IN		Electronics In progress	B

	Branch of Service	Date Entered Service	Date of Discharge	Highest Rank Held	Service-Related Skills and Experience Applicable to Civilian Employment
MILITARY SERVICE	United States Air Force	6-2-99	4-15-03	A/1C Airman First Class	Radio and small electronics repair

What experience or training have you had other than your work experience, military service and education? (Community activities, hobbies, etc.) _____

I am interested in the type of work I have checked:

Sales **✓**   Office _____   Mechanical _____   Warehouse _____   Other (Specify): **Repair**

Or the following specific job _____

I am seeking (check only one):

_____ Temporary employment (6 days or less)

_____ Seasonal employment (one season, e.g. Christmas)

✓ Regular employment (employment for indefinite period of time)

I am available for (check only one):

_____ Part-Time

✓ Full-Time Work

If part-time, indicate maximum hours per week and enter hours available in block to the right.

If temporary, indicate dates available _____

Have you been convicted during the past seven years of a serious crime involving a person's life or property?

NO **✓** YES _____ If yes, explain: _____

HOURS AVAILABLE FOR WORK		
Sunday	8 a.m.	To close
Monday	8 a.m.	To close
Tuesday	8 a.m.	To close
Wednesday	8 a.m.	To close
Thursday	8 a.m.	To close
Friday	8 a.m.	To close
Saturday	8 a.m.	To close

(continued)

(continued)

REFERENCES

LIST BELOW YOUR FOUR MOST RECENT EMPLOYERS, BEGINNING WITH THE CURRENT OR MOST RECENT ONE. IF YOU HAVE HAD FEWER THAN FOUR EMPLOYERS, USE THE REMAINING SPACES FOR PERSONAL REFERENCES. IF YOU WERE EMPLOYED UNDER A MAIDEN OR OTHER NAME, PLEASE ENTER THAT NAME IN THE RIGHT HAND MARGIN. IF APPLICABLE, ENTER SERVICE IN THE ARMED FORCES ON THE REVERSE SIDE.

NAMES AND ADDRESSES OF FORMER EMPLOYERS BEGINNING WITH THE CURRENT OR MOST RECENT	Nature of Employer's Business	Name of Your Supervisor	What kind of work did you do?	Starting Date	Starting Pay	Date of Leaving	Pay at Leaving	Why did you leave? Give details
Name Fred Willis Address 1275 E. 11th St. Tel. No. 555-2111 City Scranton State PA Zip Code 18515	Electrical subcontractor	Rafael Castillo	Electrician helper	Month 8 Year 05	$280 Per Week	Month Present Year	$280 Per Week	Work slowdown— limited work schedule
Name Scranton Public Schools Address 593 Walnut Ave. Tel. No. 555-3111 City Scranton State PA Zip Code 18505	Maintenance of school	Eric Burgess	Custodian	Month 7 Year 04	$260 Per Week	Month 3 Year 05	$260 Per Week	Desired a more demanding position
Name Grand Forks Air Force Base–USAF Address Hwy 2 Tel. No. 701-597-2112 City Grand Forks State ND Zip Code 58211	U.S. Air Force	Technical Sergeant Denise Hager	Small electronics + radio repair	Month 6 Year 99	$250 Per Week	Month 4 Year 03	$215 Per Week	Term of service expired – Honorable Discharge
Name Wayne Construction Address 1436 N. Anderson Dr. Tel. No. 555-4141 City Scranton State PA Zip Code 18509	Heavy + light constr.	Kim Lenski	Electronic equipment installer	Month 6 Year 98	$240 Per Week	Month 4 Year 99	$250 Per Week	Company went out of business—joined U.S. Air Force

NOTE: State reason for and length of inactivity between present application date and last employer. Did odd/independent jobs, college courses – 5 months

NOTE: State reason for and length of inactivity between present application date and last employer.

NOTE: State reason for and length of inactivity between present application date and last employer. Completed basic training + electronics repair school – 6 mos.

NOTE: State reason for and length of inactivity between present application date and last employer.

I certify that the information in this application is correct to the best of my knowledge and understand that any misstatement or omission of information is grounds for dismissal in accordance with Brown's policy. I authorize the references listed above to give you any and all information concerning my previous employment and any pertinent information they may have, personal or otherwise, and release all parties from all liability for any damage that may result from furnishing same to you. In consideration of my employment, I agree to conform to the rules and regulations of Brown's, and my employment and compensation can be terminated with or without cause, and with or without notice, at any time, at the option of either the Company or myself. I understand that no unit manager or representative of Brown's other than the President or Vice-President of the company, has any authority to enter into any agreement for employment for any specified period of time, or to make any agreement contrary to the foregoing. In some states, the law requires that Brown's have my written permission before obtaining consumer reports on me, and I hereby authorize Brown's to obtain such reports.

Applicant's Signature _Albert C. Smith_

NOT TO BE FILLED OUT BY APPLICANT

(Store will enter dates as required.)

		Mailed	Completed
REFERENCE REQUESTS			
CONSUMER REPORT			
With Tax (W-4)			
State With Tax			

Tested		
Physical examination scheduled for		
Physical examination form completed		
Review Card prepared	Minor's Work Permit	
Timecard prepared	Proof of Birth	
	Training Material Given to Employee	

INTERVIEWER'S COMMENTS

Date of Emp.		
Dept or Div.	Regular ___ Part-time ___	
Job Title	Job Code	
Job Title Code	Grade	
Compensation Arrangement		
Manager Approving		
Employee No.	Rack No.	

Prospect for
1.
2.

Unit Name and Number _____

Tips on Completing Applications

You've seen the difference an application can make in impressing an employer. Be sure to use the following tips as you complete your application:

You can make only one first impression, so let it be positive.

- ✔ Use your *Data Minder* to find the details needed on your application.

- ✔ Follow the instructions. Read each section carefully before completing it.

- ✔ Use an erasable black pen.

- ✔ Take your time, and avoid crossouts.

- ✔ Be accurate. Do not guess at an answer.

- ✔ Fill in every blank. Use NA (not applicable) or a short dash when something does not apply to you.

- ✔ Be honest. Being dishonest could lead to dismissal from a job. Don't include negative information, though.

- ✔ Write clearly and neatly. You can make only one impression, so make it a good one.

- ✔ Emphasize your skills and accomplishments. Find a place to mention your strengths even if the application does not ask for them.

- ✔ If you are short on paid work experience, mention your volunteer work and related hobbies under the Former Employers section.

- ✔ Get permission before using a reference.

- ✔ Sign the application if requested.

> ❝No matter how good you get you can always get better and that's the exciting part.❞
>
> *Tiger Woods*

YOUR TURN

Evaluating a Job Application

Look at the following application and decide whether you, as an employer, are impressed with the applicant.

	Yes	No
Did the applicant follow the instructions?	☐	☐
Was the applicant's writing neat?	☐	☐
Did the applicant avoid crossouts?	☐	☐
Did the applicant fill in every blank?	☐	☐
Did the applicant use NA (not applicable) or a short dash when something did not apply?	☐	☐
Did the applicant find a place to mention his strengths even if the application did not ask for them?	☐	☐
Did the applicant sign and date the application?	☐	☐

APPLICATION FOR EMPLOYMENT
(Pre-Employment Questionnaire)   (An Equal Opportunity Employer)

A. PERSONAL INFORMATION

DATE __11 - 6 - XX__

SOCIAL SECURITY NUMBER __000 - 00 - 0000__

NAME __Hired__ __Robert__ __Brian__
LAST   FIRST   MIDDLE

PRESENT ADDRESS __37 Main Street__ __Anytown__ __Utah__ __55555__
STREET   CITY   STATE   ZIP

PERMANENT ADDRESS __37 Main Street__ __Anytown__ __Utah__ __55555__
STREET   CITY   STATE   ZIP

PHONE NO. __(555) 555-0000__   ARE YOU 18 YEARS OR OLDER? ☒ YES ☐ NO

ARE YOU EITHER A U.S. CITIZEN OR AN ALIEN AUTHORIZED TO WORK IN THE UNITED STATES? ☒ YES ☐ NO

B. EMPLOYMENT DESIRED

POSITION __Security__   DATE YOU CAN START __immediately__ SALARY DESIRED __open__

ARE YOU EMPLOYED NOW? __yes__   IF SO, MAY WE INQUIRE OF YOUR PRESENT EMPLOYER? __yes__

EVER APPLIED TO THIS COMPANY BEFORE? __no__ WHERE? __—__ WHEN? __—__

REFERRED BY __Mr. George Ward__

C. EDUCATION	NAME AND LOCATION OF SCHOOL		NO. OF YEARS ATTENDED	DID YOU GRADUATE?	SUBJECTS STUDIED
GRAMMAR SCHOOL	Main Street Elem. Anytown, UT	Town Center Middle School Anytown, UT	9 yrs. (gr. K-8th)	yes	general
HIGH SCHOOL	Center High School Anytown, UT		2 yrs. (gr. 9-10th)	will graduate 6/xx	general
COLLEGE	n/a		—	—	—
TRADE, BUSINESS, OR CORRESPONDENCE SCHOOL	County J.V.S. Anytown, UT		2 yrs. (gr. 11th-12th)	will graduate 6/xx	Criminal Justice

D. GENERAL

SUBJECTS OF SPECIAL STUDY OR RESEARCH WORK __Senior in a two-year vocational Criminal Justice program. Receiving over 1500 hours of hands-on training.__

SPECIAL SKILLS __Certified in CPR. Trained in patrolling, dispatching, radio__ ✱

ACTIVITIES (CIVIC, ATHLETIC, ETC.) __Vocational Industrial Clubs of America (2 years)__
EXCLUDE ORGANIZATIONS, THE NAME OF WHICH INDICATES THE RACE, CREED, SEX, AGE, MARITAL STATUS, COLOR, OR NATION OF ORIGIN OF ITS MEMBERS.

U.S. MILITARY OR NAVAL SERVICE __n/a__ RANK __—__   PRESENT MEMBERSHIP IN NATIONAL GUARD OR RESERVES __—__

✱ __communications, arrest procedures, self-defense, and computer operations.__

(continued)

(continued)

E. FORMER EMPLOYERS. LIST BELOW LAST FOUR EMPLOYERS, STARTING WITH LAST ONE FIRST.

DATE MONTH AND YEAR	NAME AND ADDRESS OF EMPLOYER	SALARY	POSITION	REASON FOR LEAVING
FROM 6-XX TO present	IGA 300 West St., Nearby, UT	5\frac{15}{}$	customer service	n/a
FROM 11-XX TO 6-XX	McDonald's 1005 East St., Local, UT	4\frac{75}{}$	crew member	scheduling
FROM 5-XX TO 9-XX	The Smith Family 919 Park St., Local, UT	15\frac{00}{}$	lawn care	seasonal
FROM TO				

F. REFERENCES. GIVE THE NAMES OF THREE PERSONS NOT RELATED TO YOU, WHOM YOU HAVE KNOWN AT LEAST ONE YEAR.

NAME	PHONE NUMBER	BUSINESS	YEARS ACQUAINTED
1. Mr. George Ward	(555) 555-2222	Vocational Instructor at County J.V.S.	2
2. Mr. John Rocklin	(555) 555-3333	Retired GM Worker	3
3. Mrs. Susan Hughes	(555) 555-4444	Manager at McDonald's	1½

G. PHYSICAL RECORD

DO YOU HAVE ANY PHYSICAL LIMITATIONS THAT PRECLUDE YOU FROM PERFORMING ANY WORK FOR WHICH YOU ARE BEING CONSIDERED? ☐ YES ☒ NO   IF YES, WHAT CAN BE DONE TO ACCOMMODATE YOUR LIMITATION?

n/a

IN CASE OF EMERGENCY, NOTIFY Grace Hired   37 Main Street Anytown, UT 55555   (555) 555-0000
NAME (mother)   ADDRESS   PHONE NO.

"I CERTIFY THAT THE FACTS CONTAINED IN THIS APPLICATION ARE TRUE AND COMPLETE TO THE BEST OF MY KNOWLEDGE AND UNDERSTAND THAT, IF EMPLOYED, FALSIFIED STATEMENTS ON THIS APPLICATION SHALL BE GROUNDS FOR DISMISSAL.

I AUTHORIZE INVESTIGATION OF ALL STATEMENTS CONTAINED HEREIN AND THE REFERENCES LISTED ABOVE TO GIVE YOU ANY AND ALL INFORMATION CONCERNING MY PREVIOUS EMPLOYMENT AND ANY PERTINENT INFORMATION THEY MAY HAVE, PERSONAL OR OTHERWISE, AND RELEASE ALL PARTIES FROM ALL LIABILITY FOR ANY DAMAGE THAT MAY RESULT FROM FURNISHING SAME TO YOU.

I UNDERSTAND AND AGREE THAT, IF HIRED, MY EMPLOYMENT IS FOR NO DEFINITE PERIOD AND MAY, REGARDLESS OF THE DATE OF PAYMENT OF MY WAGES AND SALARY, BE TERMINATED AT ANY TIME WITHOUT ANY PRIOR NOTICE."

DATE 11-6-XX   SIGNATURE Robert B. Hired

DO NOT WRITE BELOW THIS LINE

INTERVIEWED BY _____   DATE _____

_____

_____

_____

HIRED ☐ YES ☐ NO   POSITION _____ DEPT. _____

SALARY/WAGE _____ DATE REPORTING TO WORK _____

APPROVED: 1. _____   2. _____   3. _____
EMPLOYMENT MANAGER   DEPT. HEAD   GENERAL MANAGER

ACTIVITY

Complete a Sample Job Application

Now you are ready to complete an application. In completing your own application, be as neat and as thorough as possible. You have already gathered much of the information you need in earlier chapters and in your *Data Minder*. Refer to them as needed.

An application may not get you a job, but it can get you screened out of being interviewed for one. Look over the completed application that follows. It will give you an idea of how to complete one. Then complete the blank application and remember to

✔ Use your *Data Minder* to find the details you need on your application.

✔ Act as if you were completing this application to get the job that you really want. Good luck!

(continued)

"Each time you are honest and conduct yourself with honesty, a success force will drive you toward greater success. Each time you lie, even with a little white lie, there are strong forces pushing you toward failure."

Joseph Sugarman

(continued)

Application for Employment

(Pre-Employment Questionnaire)   (An Equal Opportunity Employer)

A. PERSONAL INFORMATION

DATE _____

SOCIAL SECURITY
NUMBER _____

NAME _____
      LAST   FIRST   MIDDLE

PRESENT ADDRESS _____
              STREET   CITY   STATE   ZIP

PERMANENT ADDRESS _____
              STREET   CITY   STATE   ZIP

PHONE NO._____ ARE YOU 18 YEARS OR OLDER? ☐ YES ☐ NO

ARE YOU EITHER A U.S. CITIZEN OR AN ALIEN AUTHORIZED TO WORK IN THE UNITED STATES?
                                                              ☐ YES ☐ NO

B. EMPLOYMENT DESIRED

POSITION _____ DATE YOU CAN START _____ SALARY DESIRED _____

ARE YOU EMPLOYED NOW?_____ IF SO, MAY WE INQUIRE OF YOUR PRESENT EMPLOYER? _____

EVER APPLIED TO THIS COMPANY BEFORE? _____ WHERE? _____ WHEN?_____

REFERRED BY _____

C. EDUCATION	NAME AND LOCATION OF SCHOOL	NO. OF YEARS ATTENDED	DID YOU GRADUATE?	SUBJECTS STUDIED
GRAMMAR SCHOOL				
HIGH SCHOOL				
COLLEGE				
TRADE, BUSINESS, OR CORRESPONDENCE SCHOOL				

D. GENERAL

SUBJECTS OF SPECIAL STUDY OR RESEARCH WORK _____

_____

SPECIAL SKILLS _____

ACTIVITIES (CIVIC, ATHLETIC, ETC.) _____
EXCLUDE ORGANIZATIONS, THE NAME OF WHICH INDICATES THE RACE, CREED, SEX, AGE, MARITAL STATUS, COLOR, OR NATION OF ORIGIN OF ITS MEMBERS.

U.S. MILITARY OR   PRESENT MEMBERSHIP IN NATIONAL
NAVAL SERVICE_____ RANK_____ GUARD OR RESERVES _____

E. FORMER EMPLOYERS. LIST BELOW LAST FOUR EMPLOYERS, STARTING WITH LAST ONE FIRST.

DATE MONTH AND YEAR		NAME AND ADDRESS OF EMPLOYER	SALARY	POSITION	REASON FOR LEAVING
FROM					
TO					
FROM					
TO					
FROM					
TO					
FROM					
TO					

F. REFERENCES. GIVE THE NAMES OF THREE PERSONS NOT RELATED TO YOU, WHOM YOU HAVE KNOWN AT LEAST ONE YEAR.

NAME	PHONE NUMBER	BUSINESS	YEARS ACQUAINTED
1.			
2.			
3.			

G. PHYSICAL RECORD

DO YOU HAVE ANY PHYSICAL LIMITATIONS THAT PRECLUDE YOU FROM PERFORMING ANY WORK FOR WHICH YOU ARE BEING CONSIDERED? ☐ YES ☐ NO   IF YES, WHAT CAN BE DONE TO ACCOMMODATE YOUR LIMITATION?

_____

_____

IN CASE OF EMERGENCY, NOTIFY _____
NAME   ADDRESS   PHONE NO.

"I CERTIFY THAT THE FACTS CONTAINED IN THIS APPLICATION ARE TRUE AND COMPLETE TO THE BEST OF MY KNOWLEDGE AND UNDERSTAND THAT, IF EMPLOYED, FALSIFIED STATEMENTS ON THIS APPLICATION SHALL BE GROUNDS FOR DISMISSAL.

I AUTHORIZE INVESTIGATION OF ALL STATEMENTS CONTAINED HEREIN AND THE REFERENCES LISTED ABOVE TO GIVE YOU ANY AND ALL INFORMATION CONCERNING MY PREVIOUS EMPLOYMENT AND ANY PERTINENT INFORMATION THEY MAY HAVE, PERSONAL OR OTHERWISE, AND RELEASE ALL PARTIES FROM ALL LIABILITY FOR ANY DAMAGE THAT MAY RESULT FROM FURNISHING SAME TO YOU.

I UNDERSTAND AND AGREE THAT, IF HIRED, MY EMPLOYMENT IS FOR NO DEFINITE PERIOD AND MAY, REGARDLESS OF THE DATE OF PAYMENT OF MY WAGES AND SALARY, BE TERMINATED AT ANY TIME WITHOUT ANY PRIOR NOTICE."

DATE _____ SIGNATURE _____

DO NOT WRITE BELOW THIS LINE

INTERVIEWED BY _____ DATE _____

_____

_____

HIRED ☐ YES ☐ NO   POSITION _____ DEPT._____

SALARY/WAGE _____ DATE REPORTING TO WORK_____

APPROVED: 1. _____ 2. _____ 3. _____
EMPLOYMENT MANAGER   DEPT. HEAD   GENERAL MANAGER

Computer-Based Applications

Many employers use computer-based applications instead of paper applications because they are a more efficient way to gather information about you. Computer-based applications are filled out on a computer at the employer's office or on the Internet. These applications ask for the same information that paper applications do, so most of the guidelines for filling them out are the same. Keep the following rules in mind when you fill out computer-based applications:

✔ Make sure your spelling, grammar, and capitalization are correct.

✔ Have your *Data Minder* with you at the computer so that you'll have all the information you need.

✔ If you are completing the electronic application at the potential employer's location, ask the staff there how to use the system if you are unsure.

✔ Take your time. Read the directions carefully, fill in all of the required information, and double-check your work.

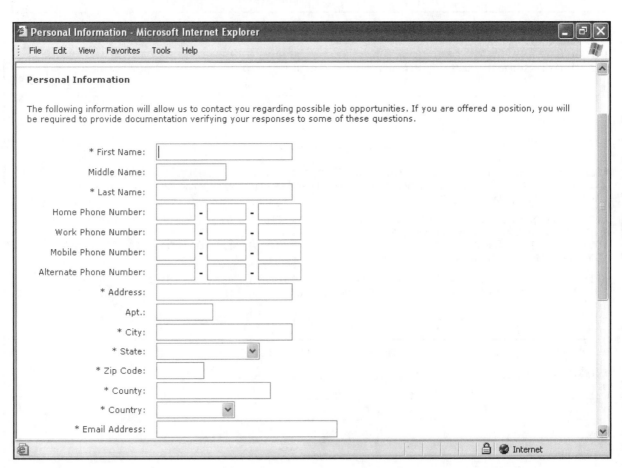

Chapter 11

Improve Your Interview Skills

Few people get a job without an interview. The interview is a crucial part of the job search process. It gives employers the chance to get to know you and you the chance to get to know them.

The Interview and Employer's Expectations

Employers use an interview to evaluate you. Will you be able to do the job? Will you be a good employee? If employers don't believe you are qualified and willing to work hard, you won't get a job offer. But if you do well in the interview, you are much more likely to get a job offer—or a referral. That's why you need to know what to do and say in a job interview. You looked at employer expectations in Chapter 2. Because they are so important, let's review them again here.

Expectation 1: Appearance (Or, Do You Look Like the Right Person?)

Remember that employers will react to first impressions. The way you come across in the first few minutes is very important.

If you do well in the interview, you are more likely to get a job offer.

- ✔ **Personal appearance:** If you do not look like the right person or if your appearance is "wrong," an employer will be turned off immediately.

- ✔ **Manner:** Arrive early and be relaxed. Be polite with the receptionist or other staff. Greet the employer in a friendly way, and shake hands if offered. During the interview, be aware of how you look to the interviewer. For example, leaning forward a bit in your chair helps you look interested and alert. Smiling and looking at the interviewer as he speaks helps you seem more confident.

✔ **Paperwork:** Your application, JIST Card, resume, and portfolio create an impression. Are they neat, error free, accurate, and filled out completely?

✔ **Communications:** Speak in a distinct, clear voice. Use proper grammar. Emphasize the things you can do well and a willingness to try hard. Be honest and open with your answers.

Expectation 2: Attendance, Punctuality, and Reliability (Or, Can You Be Counted On?)

Remember that all employers want someone they can depend on. Keep these points in mind:

✔ **Daily attendance and punctuality:** Be early for the interview. Mention your good attendance record at school or other jobs.

✔ **Dependability:** Employers want to hire people they can trust to do the job. Many questions that employers ask during interviews will give you a chance to show that you are reliable. Give some examples demonstrating your reliability.

Expectation 3: Skills, Experience, and Training (Or, Can You Do the Job?)

Emphasize what you can do. Think in advance what the job requires, and emphasize points that support your doing it well.

Be sure to emphasize your skills.

✔ **Skills:** Employers will want to know your skills. Review your skills lists from Chapter 3 to remind yourself what you can do. Because you will probably compete with job seekers who have more work experience, emphasize your self-management and transferable skills in your interview responses.

Other points to discuss include the following:

✔ Experience

✔ Life experience

✔ Education and training

✔ Achievements

✔ Interests and hobbies

Remember: Employers Are Evaluating You

In one way or another, interviewers must find out about all the preceding issues. At every point in the interview process, they are evaluating you—even when you might least expect it.

The following section breaks down the interview into six phases. As you learn to handle each one, you will be better able to meet an employer's expectations. Then you will be much more likely to get a job offer.

Six Phases of an Interview

No two interviews are alike, but there are similarities. If you look closely at the interview process, you can see separate phases. Looking at each phase will help you learn how to handle interviews well. The phases are as follows:

1. Before the interview

2. Opening moves

3. The interview itself

4. Closing the interview

5. Following up

6. Making a final decision

Every step of the interview is important. The following sections show you why and give you tips for handling each phase.

Phase 1: Before the Interview

An interviewer can make judgments about you in many ways before you meet. For example, you may have spoken to the interviewer or the interviewer's assistant on the phone. You may have sent the interviewer a resume or other correspondence via e-mail or postal mail. Or someone may have told the interviewer about you.

 TIP Be careful in all your early contacts with an employer. Do everything possible to create a good impression.

Before you meet an interviewer, here are some things to consider.

Dress and Grooming

The way you dress and groom for an interview varies from job to job. You will have to make your own decisions about what is right for each interview situation. Because there are so many differences, there are no firm rules on how to dress. But you should avoid certain things. Here are some important tips:

- ✔ Don't wear jeans, tank tops, shorts, or other casual clothes.

- ✔ Be conservative. An interview is not a good time to be trendy.

- ✔ Check your shoes. Little things count, so pay attention to everything you wear.

- ✔ Be conservative with cologne, aftershave, makeup, and jewelry.

- ✔ Careful grooming is a must. Get those hands and nails extra clean and manicured. Eliminate stray facial hairs.

- ✔ Spend some money if necessary. Get one well-fitting interview outfit.

Research on the Company

Know as much as you can about the organization before you go to an important interview. Find out about the following:

- ✔ **The organization**

  - ∗ Major products or services

  - ∗ Number of employees

  - ∗ Reputation

  - ∗ Values

- ✔ **The position**

  - ∗ Existing openings, if any

  - ∗ Salary range and benefits

  - ∗ Duties and responsibilities

Punctuality

Get to the interview a few minutes early. Make sure you know how to get there, and allow plenty of time. Call for directions if necessary.

Final Grooming

Before you go in for the interview, stop in a rest room. Look at yourself in a mirror and make any final adjustments.

Waiting Room Behavior

Assume that interviewers will hear about everything you do in the waiting room. They will ask the receptionist how you conducted yourself—and how you treated the receptionist.

Courtesy Toward the Receptionist

The receptionist's opinion of you matters. Go out of your way to be polite and friendly. If you spoke to the receptionist on the phone, mention that and express appreciation for any help you were offered.

Delay Because of the Interviewer

If the interviewer is late, you are lucky. The interviewer will probably feel bad about keeping you waiting and may give you better-than-average treatment to make up for it.

If you have to wait more than 20 minutes or so, ask to reschedule your appointment. You don't want to act as if you have nothing to do. And, again, the interviewer may make it up to you later.

Phase 2: Opening Moves

The first few minutes of an interview are critical. If you make a bad impression, you probably won't be able to change it. Interviewers react to many things you say and do during the first few minutes of an interview. Here are some points they mention most often.

Initial Greeting

Be ready for a friendly greeting. Show that you are happy to be there. Although this is a business meeting, your social skills will be considered. If the interviewer offers to shake hands, give him a firm, but not crushing handshake.

Posture

The way you stand and sit can make a difference. You look more interested if you lean forward in your chair when talking or listening. If you lean back, you may look *too* relaxed.

Voice

You may be nervous, but try to sound enthusiastic. Your voice should be neither too soft nor too loud.

TIP Practice sounding confident. It will help you feel confident.

Eye Contact

People who don't look in the speaker's eyes are considered shy, insecure, and even dishonest. Although you should never stare, you seem more confident when you look in the interviewer's eyes while you listen or speak.

Distracting Habits

You may have nervous habits you don't even notice. But pay attention! Most interviewers find such habits annoying. For example, do you play with your hair or say something like "you know" over and over? (You know what I mean?)

The best way to see yourself as others do is to have someone videotape you while you role-play an interview. If that is not possible, become aware of how others see you and try to change negative behavior.

TIP Your friends and relatives can point out annoying habits you have that could bother an interviewer.

Establishing the Relationship

Almost all interviews begin with informal small talk. Favorite subjects are the weather and whether you had trouble getting there. This chatting seems to have nothing to do with the interview. But it does. These first few minutes allow an interviewer to relax you and find out how you relate to each other.

You can do many things during the first few minutes of an interview. The following are some suggestions from experienced interviewers:

✔ **Allow things to happen:** Relax. Don't feel you have to start a serious interview right away.

✔ **Smile:** Look happy to be there and to meet the interviewer.

✔ **Use the interviewer's name:** Be formal. Use "Mr. Stewart" or "Ms. Evans" unless you are asked to use another name. Use the interviewer's name as often as you can in your conversation.

Phase 3: The Interview Itself

This is the most complex part of the interview. It can last from 15 to 45 minutes or more while the interviewer tries to find your strengths and weaknesses.

Interviewers may ask you almost anything. They are looking for any problems you may have. They also want to be convinced that you have the skills, experience, and personality to do a good job. If you have made a good impression so far, you can use this phase to talk about your qualifications.

> **TIP**
>
> You will learn how to create a career portfolio in Chapter 12. Take this portfolio with you to the interview and present it to the employer. Be sure to point out its most relevant and impressive elements. Leave copies of these items with the employer.

How to Answer Problem Questions

In one survey, employers said that more than 90 percent of the people they interviewed could not answer problem questions. More than 80 percent could not explain the skills they had for the job. This is a serious problem for most job seekers. It keeps many of them from getting a good job that will use their skills.

Interviewers may ask you almost anything.

There are hundreds of questions an interviewer might ask you in an interview. It would be impossible for you to have answers prepared for all of them. A better approach is to learn a technique to answering most interview questions.

Three Steps to Answering Problem Questions

Answering problem questions is never easy, but you can do it with more confidence if you know the following three steps:

1. **Understand what is really being asked.**

   Most employers are trying to find out about your self-management skills. While rarely this blunt, the employer's real questions are often the following:

   * Can I depend on you?

   * Are you easy to get along with?

   * Are you a good worker?

The question may also be the following:

* Do you have the experience and training to do the job if I hire you?

2. **Answer the question briefly.**

* Acknowledge the facts, but...

* Present them as an advantage, not a disadvantage.

3. **Answer the real concern by presenting your related skills.**

* Base your answer on your key skills from your lists in Chapter 3.

* Give examples to support your skills statements.

> "*No bird soars too high if he soars with his own wings.*"
>
> William Blake

ACTIVITY

Answer Problem Questions

This activity will help you form answers to the most common problem interview questions. Here are a few pointers:

✔ Write out complete and honest answers for each question.

✔ Suggestions are included to help you prepare answers that will stand out and impress employers. Don't forget to give lots of examples.

✔ A good answer should take between 30 seconds and two minutes.

✔ Sell yourself!

PROBLEM QUESTIONS WORKSHEET

1. Can you tell me a little about yourself?

Suggestions

Talk about your education: when you're graduating, what you're majoring in, and what your achievements are.

Talk about your experience in both related and unrelated jobs.

Talk about your good-worker traits.

_____

_____

_____

_____

_____

_____

(continued)

(continued)

2. Why are you applying for this type of job, and why here?_____

Suggestions

You discovered through training that you enjoy and are good at this type of work.

You noticed the company's ad; got a referral from someone; know the company has an excellent reputation; and so on.

_____
_____
_____
_____
_____
_____
_____

3. What training or experience qualifies you for this position?_____

Suggestions

Refer to Chapter 4 and your *Data Minder* pages 4–15 and 21.

_____
_____
_____
_____

4. What are the greatest strengths you would bring to this job?_____

Suggestions

Refer to Chapter 3 and *Data Minder* pages 7 and 21 for your job-related, self-management, and transferable skills.

Talk about your best skills, and use examples to prove them.

_____
_____
_____
_____
_____
_____

5. What do you consider your greatest weakness?_____

_____

_____

Suggestions

Never say that you don't have weaknesses or that you cannot think of any.

Never talk about a weakness that will prevent you from being hired.

Mention a job skill you have not learned yet or have trouble doing well.

Say something positive after you mention a weakness, such as "But I'm anxious to learn" or "But I can do such-and-such well."

Say that you tend to ask lots of questions when starting a job, but it's because you want to do your work correctly.

_____

_____

_____

_____

_____

_____

_____

_____

6. How much do you expect to be paid?_____

Suggestions

Research pay rates by talking with people in the profession.

Give a range, such as between $6 and $8 per hour.

Ask if new employees have a trial period, how long it lasts, and what happens when it ends. Possibilities include the job becoming full time, salary increasing, or benefits being added.

_____

_____

_____

_____

_____

_____

_____

(continued)

(continued)

7. Can you tell me about a problem you had on your previous job and how you handled it?_____

Suggestions

This checks your ability to act maturely and professionally.

Choose an example that shows you handled a situation well.

_____
_____
_____
_____

8. How can you help us make more money or do better as an organization?

Suggestions

Say that you can help by being a highly dependable employee.

Give your definition of dependability: being on time and at work every day; being early and willing to stay late; and getting your work done well and on time.

_____
_____
_____
_____
_____

9. What would you consider your ideal job?_____

Suggestions

Be realistic.

Make sure your answer reflects stability. Employers are looking for people who will stay for at least two years to be worth their training time and effort.

_____
_____
_____
_____
_____

10. Can you tell me why you consider yourself a responsible person?_____

Suggestions

Refer to Chapter 2 on employer expectations.

Give several examples that show you are a reliable person.

_____
_____
_____
_____

11. What are your interests and preferred activities?_____

Suggestions

Refer to your *Data Minder* pages 5, 14–15.

_____

_____

_____

12. Why should I offer you the job?_____

Suggestions

State that you feel you are well qualified.

State that you have the necessary qualifications, such as the following:

Training: I have two years of intensive vocational training in an automotive repair program with more than 1,500 hours of hands-on experience.

Education: I have a vocational certificate and high school diploma.

Experience: Talk about your jobs, how long you held them, and what you learned.

Skills: Mention eight or more skills that you do well, that would be necessary for the job, and that would impress the employer.

_____

_____

_____

_____

_____

_____

_____

_____

_____

_____

_____

_____

50 More Problem Questions

The following questions came from a survey of 92 companies that conduct student interviews. Look for questions you would have trouble answering. Then practice answering them using the three-step process.

1. In what school activities have you participated? Why? Which do you enjoy the most?

2. How do you spend your spare time? What are your hobbies?

3. Why do you think you might like to work for our company?

4. What jobs have you held? How did you obtain them, and why did you leave?

5. What courses did you like best? Least? Why?

6. Why did you choose your particular field of work?

7. What percentage of your school expense did you earn? How?

8. What do you know about our company?

9. Do you feel that you have received good general training?

10. What qualifications do you have that make you feel that you will be successful in your field?

11. What are your ideas on salary?

12. If you were starting school all over again, what courses would you take?

13. Can you forget your education and start from scratch?

14. How much money do you hope to earn at age 25? 30? 40?

15. Why did you decide to go to the school you attended?

16. What was your rank in your graduating class in high school? Other schools?

17. Do you think that your extracurricular activities were worth the time you devoted to them? Why?

18. What personal characteristics are necessary for success in your chosen field?

19. Why do you think you would like this particular type of job?

20. Are you looking for a permanent or a temporary job?

21. Are you primarily interested in making money, or do you feel that service to your fellow human beings is a satisfactory accomplishment?

22. Do you prefer working with others or by yourself?

23. Can you take instructions without feeling upset?

24. Tell me a story!

25. What have you learned from some of the jobs you have held?

26. Can you get recommendations from previous employers?

27. What interests you about our product or service?

28. What was your record in the military service?

29. What do you know about opportunities in the field in which you are trained?

30. How long do you expect to work for us?

31. Have you ever had difficulty getting along with fellow students and faculty? Fellow workers?

32. Which of your school years was most difficult?

33. Do you like routine work?

34. Do you like work with the same days and hours, or are you willing to work flexible days and hours?

35. In what area do you need the most improvement?

36. Define cooperation.

37. Will you fight to get ahead?

38. Do you have an analytical mind?

39. Are you willing to go where the company sends you?

40. What job in our company would you choose if you were entirely free to do so?

41. Do you have plans for further education?

42. What jobs have you enjoyed the most? The least? Why?

(continued)

43. What are your own special abilities?

44. What job in our company do you want to work toward?

45. Would you prefer a large or a small company? Why?

46. How do you feel about overtime work?

47. What kind of work interests you?

48. Do you think that employers should consider grades?

49. What obstacles have you overcome?

50. What have you done that shows initiative and willingness to work?

Questions You Might Ask an Employer

Most interviewers will invite you to ask questions about the job or organization. The following are questions you can ask during the interview and questions to ask when offered the job.

During the interview:

✔ Is there a trial period for new employees? How long is it?

✔ Are there opportunities for additional training and schooling?

✔ What tools and equipment are used in this job?

✔ Is a uniform required?

✔ How is an employee promoted?

✔ Could you give me a tour?

> "No one can make you feel inferior without your consent."
>
> *Eleanor Roosevelt*

YOUR TURN

List Other Questions You Can Ask

List other questions you can ask to demonstrate your interest in doing well.

_____

_____

_____

_____

_____

_____

When offered the job:

Employers are interested in what you can do for them, not what you want from them. For this reason, it is often wise to avoid certain questions until you're offered the job. Examples include questions related to salary, vacations, and benefits.

Phase 4: Closing the Interview

You can close an interview as effectively as you began it. Most people are not offered the job at the close of the first interview. However, you can take certain steps to make a good impression.

Summarize at the Finish

Take a few minutes to summarize the key points of the interview. If any problems or weaknesses came up, state why they will not keep you from doing a good job. Point out strengths you have for the job and why you believe you can do it well.

Ask for the Job

If you are interested in the job, say so. If you want this job, ask for it. Many employers hire one person over another just because one person really wants it and says so.

The Call-Back Close

With the call-back close, you can end the interview to your advantage. It will take some practice, and you may not be comfortable with it at first. But it works. Here's how:

1. **Thank the interviewer by name:** While shaking hands, say "Thank you (Mr. or Ms. or Mrs. Jones) for your time today."

2. **Express interest in the job and organization:** Tell the interviewer that you are interested in the position or organization (or both). For example: "The position we discussed today is just what I have been looking for. I am also very impressed with your organization."

3. **Arrange a reason and a time to call back:** If the interviewer has been helpful, he or she won't mind your following up. It's important that you arrange a day and time to call. Never expect the employer to call you. Say something like this: "I'm sure I'll have more questions. When would be the best time for me to get back to you?"

4. **Say good-bye:** After you've set a time and date to call back, thank the interviewer by name and say goodbye: "Again, thank you, Mr. Pomeroy, for the time you gave me today. I will call you next Tuesday morning between 9 and 10 o'clock."

Phase 5: Following Up

You have left the interview and it's over. Right? Not really. You need to follow up! This can make the difference between getting the job or not. Here are some things you must do:

> *Your follow-up can make the difference between getting the job or not.*

✔ **Send a thank-you note or e-mail:** As soon as possible after the interview—no later than 24 hours—send a mailed or e-mailed thank-you note. Enclose a JIST Card, too. See the information on thank-you notes at the end of this chapter.

✔ **Make notes:** Write yourself notes about the interview while it is still fresh in your mind. You will not remember details in a week or so.

✔ **Follow up as promised:** If you said you would call back next Tuesday at 9 a.m., do it. You will impress the interviewer with your organizational skills.

Phase 6: Making a Final Decision

The interview process is not over until you accept a job. This can sometimes be an easy decision. At other times, deciding can be difficult. Before you accept or turn down a job, consider the following points:

✔ Responsibilities and duties of the job.

✔ Hours you will have to work.

✔ Salary and benefits.

✔ Location and how you will get there. For example, can you take a bus, or will you need a car?

✔ Working conditions.

✔ Opportunity for advancement.

After you accept a job verbally, write an acceptance letter that confirms the starting date and time. Be sure to keep a copy of your letter.

Steps to Take the Evening Before Your Interview

1. Select and lay out what you plan to wear. Make sure everything is cleaned, pressed, and appropriate. Avoid flashy clothes, excessive jewelry, and strong perfume or cologne.

2. Gather and review the materials you plan to take with you. Include your career portfolio (discussed in Chapter 12), extra copies of your resume, list of references, letters of recommendation, and your *Data Minder*.

3. Make sure you know how to get there on time. Take written instructions or a map if you are not familiar with the interview's location.

4. Take a small notepad and two pens for jotting important notes from your interview.

5. Take extra money to cover unexpected expenses.

6. Get a good night's rest.

Tips for Interviewing

The person who gets a job offer is not necessarily the best qualified, but the one who makes the best impression.

- ✔ Be neat and clean from head to foot.

- ✔ Be knowledgeable about the company.

- ✔ Display a positive attitude.

- ✔ Smile and be enthusiastic.

- ✔ Listen attentively, and make direct eye contact.

- ✔ Watch your body language.

- ✔ Approach the question of salary by giving a range and by knowing the typical salary for the job.

- ✔ Don't talk too much, or you'll talk yourself out of a job.

- ✔ Arrive a few minutes early.

- ✔ Get the interviewer to like you.

- ✔ Keep looking even if you get an offer. Stop only after you have formally accepted a job.

Thank-You Notes

Sending a thank-you note is a simple act of appreciation, and most people don't take the time to do it. It is polite to send thank-you notes to employers who interview you and to anyone who helps you during your job search. If you e-mail a thank-you, consider also sending one in the mail.

Thank-you notes also have practical benefits. People who receive them will remember you. But employers say that they rarely get thank-you notes. Employers describe people who do send them with positive terms, such as thoughtful, well organized, and thorough.

A thank-you note won't get you a job you're not qualified for, but it will impress people. When a job opens up, employers will remember you. People in your job search network will also be more interested in helping you. If they know of an opening or meet someone who does, they will think of you.

Thank-You Note Examples

Carefully look at and read the following two examples of thank-you notes. Does one look more professional to you than the other? Is one more clearly written than the other?

2244 Riverwood Avenue
Philadelphia, PA 17963
April 16, 20XX

Ms. Helen A. Colcord
Henderson & Associates, Inc.
1801 Washington Blvd., Suite 1201
Philadelphia, PA 17993

Dear Ms. Colcord:

Thank you for sharing your time with me so generously today. I really appreciated seeing your state-of-the-art computer equipment.

Your advice has already proved helpful. I have an appointment to meet with Mr. Robert Hopper on Friday. As you anticipated, he does intend to add more computer operators in the next few months.

In case you think of someone else who might need a person like me, I'm enclosing another JIST Card. I will let you know how the interview with Mr. Hopper goes.

Sincerely,

William Henderson

William Henderson

Sept. 30, 20XX

Dear Mr. Hernandez,

Thank you for the interview today. I'm impressed by the high standards your department maintains — the more I heard and saw, the more interested I became in working for your firm.

As we agreed, I will call you next Monday, Oct. 5. In the meantime, please call if you have additional questions.

Sincerely,
Kay Howell

Tips for Preparing Thank-You Notes

Here are some tips for preparing thank-you notes:

✔ **Paper and envelope:** Use good-quality notepaper with matching envelopes. Most stationery stores, card shops, and office-supply stores have these supplies. Avoid cute designs. Notepaper with a simple "Thank You" on the front will do. Off-white and buff colors are good.

✔ **Typed versus handwritten:** You do not always have to send a formal, typed thank-you letter. Handwritten notes are fine unless your handwriting is illegible or sloppy. A neat, written note can be very effective.

✔ **Salutation:** Unless you are thanking a friend or relative, don't use first names. Write "Dear Ms. Krenshaw" rather than "Dear Lisa." Include the date.

✔ **The note:** Keep it short and friendly. This is not the place to write, "The reason you should hire me is...." Remember that the note is a thank you for what the person did. It is not a hard-sell pitch for what you want. As appropriate, be specific about when you will next be in contact. If you plan to meet with the person soon, send a note saying you look forward to meeting again and name the date and time.

✔ **Your signature:** Use your first and last names. Avoid initials, and make your signature legible.

✔ **When to send it:** Send your note no later than 24 hours after your interview or conversation. Ideally, you should write it immediately after the contact while the details are fresh in your mind. Always send a note after an interview, even if things did not go well.

✔ **Enclosure:** Depending on the situation, a JIST Card is often the ideal enclosure. It's a soft sell that provides your phone number if the person wants to reach you. Make sure your note cards are large enough to hold your JIST Card.

YOUR TURN

Write a Thank-You Note

Writing a thank-you note takes just a few minutes. Write a thank-you note that you can use as a template for notes you will write after phone conversations or interviews with employers.

Chapter 12

Create Your Career Portfolio

Unlike a resume, a portfolio contains a variety of documents and items in print or electronic form. A career portfolio includes items such as school transcripts, writing and artwork samples, and anything else you think will be helpful in getting a good job.

A career portfolio is designed to help you make the transition from school to work. You can update the portfolio as needed and continue to use it as you seek other employment and education.

A career portfolio will help you present your skills in a format that is easy to recognize and read. For employers, colleges, and training programs, the career portfolio is a tool that helps them screen and select applicants.

The career portfolio is a tool you can use in any situation that calls for a resume or a description of skills and abilities. It gives you a better chance of getting the opportunity you want.

What Are the Benefits of a Career Portfolio?

A career portfolio benefits you in the following ways:

✔ Helps you define your skills

✔ Gives you a better understanding of what employers look for

✔ Improves your ability to market yourself

✔ Increases your confidence when interviewing

✔ Increases your chances for obtaining a good job and getting into college

What Is in a Career Portfolio?

A career portfolio can include a variety of items. Depending on your situation, here are some items you may want to place in your portfolio:

✔ Letter from principal or school superintendent

✔ Resume

✔ High school transcript

✔ Essay on your career goals

✔ Summary of skills

✔ Credentials, such as diplomas and certificates of recognition

✔ Optional items, such as writing samples and teacher recommendations

A good portfolio will improve your chances of getting the job you want.

Put each item on a separate page when you assemble your career portfolio. This chapter explains the previous list and gives examples.

Portfolios can be in print or electronic form. It might be a Web page or site where you post your information and samples of your work. If your school has or requires an electronic portfolio, your instructor will give you more information on what is needed.

Letter from Your Principal or Superintendent

The first page of the career portfolio can be a letter from your school principal or other administrator. This letter should be on school letterhead.

The letter's purpose is to confirm that you attended the school. A general letter is usually made available to all students who are preparing career portfolios through a class. If you are developing a portfolio on your own, ask your principal to write this letter for you. A sample follows.

Neighborhood High School
4444 Friendly Drive
Anytown, New York 12345

To Whom It May Concern:

The faculty of Neighborhood High School appreciates your consideration of the individual presenting this Career Portfolio. Only graduates of our high school or students in good standing have such a document. We trust that you will find this individual to have mastered the various competencies associated with a strong high school curriculum and to have been involved in various school and community activities.

We believe the information contained in this document is accurate and useful to you. In addition, we invite you to visit our high school and our classrooms and observe our commitment to excellence in education. Thank you for your continued support of our graduates and our school system. We believe you will find this individual's performance to be commensurate with the information contained within this portfolio.

Sincerely,

Principal

Resume Example

You should include the resume that you developed in Chapter 9. Here is a sample resume from one student's portfolio.

JOHN SNOW
234 Steeple Road
Anytown, North Dakota 12345
(222) 333-4444
johnsnow@connect.com

Objective

To receive a Bachelor's Degree in the biology field.

Experience

Panoli's	Ms. Joy Autumn
500 West Farm Drive	338 Bobcat Drive-Apt. C
Anytown, North Dakota 12345	Anytown, North Dakota 12345
(222) 555-6666	(222) 555-7777
June 20XX-November 20XX	November 20XX-May 20XX
Prepared food, ran cashier register,	Cared for three children and
and cleaned the establishment.	performed household duties.

Volunteer Service

Volunteered at the Animal Welfare League in Littletown. Assisted the veterinarian and performed lab work. Groomed, fed, and bathed the animals.

Education

Neighborhood High School
1222 Main Street
Anytown, North Dakota 12345
(222) 111-2222
Received Diploma – 6/XX

Have had the following College Preparatory Courses:

English (3 years)	Anatomy
History (3 years)	Geometry
Biology	Algebra I and II

Achievements

Grade Point Average 3.7 Junior year
Student of the Month for English

Personal

I am a strong person who loves a challenge, enjoys being around people, and learns quickly.

Transcript Example

The school transcript is an official document that shows the courses you have taken in high school. It includes your grades and the credits earned, grade point average, days of absences and tardiness, and test scores, and it may include community service hours completed. It should bear the school's stamp or seal plus the signature of the school administrator.

Follow your school's policy to obtain your transcript. Most employers and college representatives will ask for your transcript, so it is good to include it in your portfolio. Here is a sample transcript.

JANET M. JONES
789 Main Street
Anytown, AZ 12345
PARENT/GUARDIAN: Sue R. Jones
DATE OF BIRTH: 2-5-XX

STUDENT ID: 222-33-4444
ADMISSION DATE: August 25, 20XX
WITHDRAWAL DATE:
GRADUATION DATE: June 6, 20XX
HOMEROOM: 231
COUNSELOR: M. FRANK

COURSE TITLE	FINAL MARK	CRED EARN	COURSE TITLE	FINAL MARK	CRED EARN
YEAR: XX/XX**************GRADE:		09	YEAR: XX/XX*************GRADE:		10
ENGLISH 9	A+	1.000	ENGLISH 10	A-	1.000
GL. CULT & HIST	A	1.000	AMERICAN HISTORY	B+	1.000
ALGEBRA 1	A+	1.000	GEOMETRY	A-	1.000
BIOLOGY	A	1.000	BIOLOGY 2	A	1.000
FRENCH 1	A	1.000	FRENCH 2	A	1.000
PHYS ED 1st SEM	A+	0.250	PHYS ED 1st SEM	A	0.250
PHYS ED 2nd SEM	A-	0.250	PHYS ED 2nd SEM	A	0.250
BEG TYP & KYBD	A	1.000	INTERMED KYBD	B+	1.000
YEAR: XX/XX**************GRADE:		11	YEAR: XX/XX*************GRADE:		12
ENGLISH 11	A-	1.000	ENGLISH 12	A	1.000
CALCULUS	A	1.000	GOVERNMENT	A	1.000
CHEMISTRY	B+	1.000	TRIGONOMETRY	A-	1.000
FRENCH 3	A	1.000	PHYSICS	B	1.000
ART 1st SEM	A	0.500	FRENCH 4	A-	1.000
ART 2nd SEM	A	0.500			

YEAR	ABSENT	TARDY	MO/YR	ATTM CRED	EARN CRED	GPA
XX/XX	2.0	0	06/XX	6.500	6.500	4.000
XX/XX	3.0	1	06/XX	5.000	5.000	3.750
XX/XX	1.0	0	06/XX	5.000	5.000	3.833
XX/XX	1.0	0	06/XX	5.000	5.000	3.800

AZ PROFICIENCY TEST:	DATE PASSED		
MATHEMATICS	OCT. 25, 20XX	CREDITS ATTEMPTED	23.000
CITIZENSHIP	OCT. 25, 20XX	CREDITS EARNED	23.000
WRITING	OCT. 25, 20XX	POINTS EARNED	98.000
		GRADE POINT AVERAGE	3.846
		CLASS RANK	10th/427

VOLUNTEER COMMUNITY SERVICE
  HOURS COMPLETED: 59.5
DATE ISSUED: JUNE 22, 20XX

PRINCIPAL: Mr. Dudley DoGood
Neighborhood High School
Anytown, AZ

Essay on Career Goals Examples

You should develop a one-page essay that describes your career goals and why you decided on them. It should also explain what you plan to do after high school and a "plan B" if the next step doesn't work out. This essay is based on information about yourself. It should include things that you can prove or that you can illustrate by examples.

Your career essay gives employers another chance to know more about you and why you chose your career goals. It is important that your essay is well planned, uses correct grammar, and is in an easy-to-follow format. Type it with a word processing program, and print it on quality paper.

TIP   Make sure your career essay and other portfolio documents are neat and error free.

You may want to include the following information in your essay:

- ✔ SAT or ACT scores.

- ✔ Results of career assessments of interest and aptitude.

- ✔ A summary of experiences that directly relate to your career goal. Examples of these experiences include the following:

  - * Club memberships, such as a group for future pharmacists.

  - * Actual work experience in a related field.

  - * Community service that is relevant to your career goal.

  - * Job shadowing, internships, and mentorships in your career field.

High school students wrote the following samples. They will give you some ideas on writing your essay.

My Future Plans

With the coming of my senior year of high school, I have been thinking about what to do with my life. I take that issue seriously. Since my junior year of high school, I have been thinking of the possible job opportunities that await me. After examining the careers that suit both my talents and my interests, I have come up with a potential plan for my future.

As an A student, I enjoy attending school, helping others, and accepting challenges. For those reasons, I would like to go into the field of teaching. Mathematics seems to be my strongest subject. I have achieved a perfect grade in my math classes since entering high school, and I am currently tutoring two of my peers in this subject area. Other courses I enjoy include science, history, and government. During my senior year, I plan to take physics, calculus, a history course, and possibly an economics or psychology class at the college level through a postsecondary study program. I believe I could be successful in a teaching career for the reasons already stated and also because of my ability to learn quickly and my desire to help people achieve their goals.

If my teaching plan is for some reason unachievable, my backup plan is to go into a career dealing with financing. I should be able to excel in this career because of my strong mathematics background. Working with numbers is something I can do well, so I think it would be a good second major.

In all likelihood, I will have a double major in college so that I will have different career choices. It is too risky for me to specialize in one particular field and then discover that no jobs are available to me. Whatever I end up pursuing, I know I will do my best at the job and offer a lot to that profession.

Preparing for the Future

Graduation is quickly approaching, and I have many important decisions yet to make. I am currently planning to attend a technical school to pursue my desire of becoming a design engineer.

While in the eighth grade, my industrial arts teacher informed me that I had talent in this area and could be successful as a design engineer. Since then, I have continued to sharpen this talent and have realized that I really enjoy this field. I have taken or plan to take the following high school courses for preparation in this area: Industrial Arts I, Industrial Arts II, Algebra I, Algebra II, Geometry, Pre-Calculus with Trigonometry, and Physics. I am also computer literate and am familiar with the AutoCAD program.

If my plans to become a design engineer do not work out, I will pursue a position as a computer scientist. I enjoy using computers and believe that the computer field is an appropriate alternative career choice. If I decide to strive for this position, I will need to attend a four-year college.

With much effort and dedication, I believe I will accomplish these goals. In conclusion, the achievements that I obtain today will help me pursue a successful career.

As simple as it sounds, we all must try to be the best person we can: by making the best choices, by making the most of the talents we've been given.

Mary Lou Retton

ACTIVITY

Write Your Career Essay

Use the worksheet that follows to write a rough draft of your career essay. Your school may have different requirements for your career essay than what we've explained. Your instructor will suggest what to include if it differs from our examples.

CAREER ESSAY WORKSHEET

_____

_____

_____

_____

_____

_____

_____

_____

_____

_____

_____

_____

_____

_____

_____

_____

_____

_____

_____

_____

_____

Summary of Skills Examples

This section gives you an opportunity to summarize your job-related skills in a brief essay or to simply list them.

TIP Refer to Chapter 3 to review your job-related skills.

If you have taken vocational training courses, your teacher can help you identify the job-related skills you have mastered. Some examples of vocational training courses are keyboarding, accounting, woodshop, and drafting. You may be in a school that will provide a detailed listing of the skills learned in these courses.

Another way to summarize your skills is to write an essay that describes the good-worker traits or self-management skills you listed in Chapter 3.

The next couple of pages show samples of these different summaries.

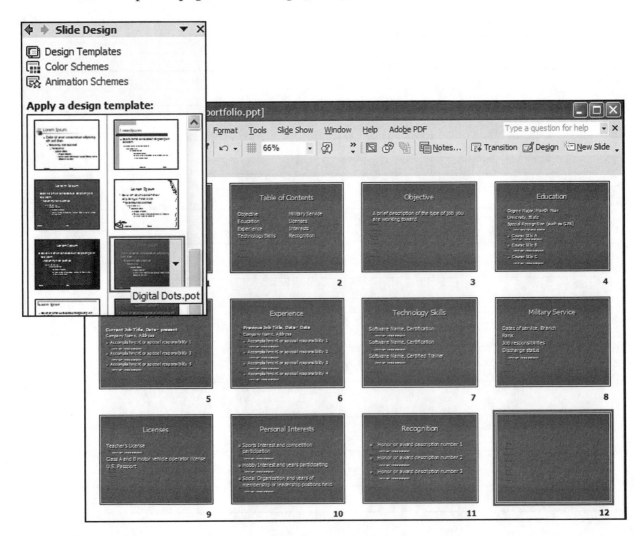

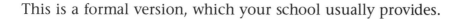

This is a formal version, which your school usually provides.

MAJOR COMPETENCY AREAS
of
JOSEPH P. GOODWRENCH

The competencies listed below are those competencies that **Joseph P. Goodwrench** has demonstrated proficiency in and can perform the complete job with normal supervision in the traditional job setting.

BASIC SKILLS

Practice safety procedures and shopkeeping
Maintain tools and equipment
Analyze metals
Cut metals
Repair fasteners
Repair electrical wiring

NONSTRUCTURAL ANALYSIS AND DAMAGE REPAIR

Prepare damaged surface
Replace and adjust outer body panel
Repair and finish steel metal surface
Apply body filling
Perform gas metal arc welding

STRUCTURAL ANALYSIS AND DAMAGE REPAIR

Repair frame
Repair unibody units according to manufacturer's specifications
Repair modular and fixed glass

PLASTICS AND ADHESIVES

Identify and repair rigid and flexible plastic parts

PAINTING AND REFINISHING

Prepare surface
Perform spray gun operations
Mix, match, and apply paint
Identify and correct finish defects
Perform detailing procedures

MECHANICAL AND ELECTRICAL COMPONENTS

Identify lubricants and fluids
Repair electrical systems
Repair brakes and automatic brake system (ABS)
Repair heating and air-conditioning (AC)
Repair cooling system
Repair drive train
Repair fuel, intake, and exhaust systems
Repair active restraint systems
Repair passive restraint systems
Repair supplemental air bag restraint systems according to manufacturer's specifications

SERVICE MANAGEMENT

Manage and operate body shop
Maintain company security requirements
Manage customer relations
Conduct training
Order parts
Prepare estimates
Prepare documentation

COMMUNICATIONS

Apply communications skills

OCCUPATIONAL SKILLS

Apply mathematical skills
Demonstrate business and work ethics

AUTO BODY—2-YEAR PROGRAM
Neighborhood Career Center

This is an example of a simple listing that you can do yourself:

JOSEPH P. GOODWRENCH

Collision Repair Skills

- ✓ Remove rust
- ✓ Repair dents
- ✓ Apply fillers
- ✓ Smooth surfaces
- ✓ Grinding
- ✓ Sanding
- ✓ Sand blasting
- ✓ Welding
- ✓ Air brushing
- ✓ Masking and painting
- ✓ Remove, repair, and replace belts, struts, batteries, rocker and quarter panels, fenders, doors, hood, and trunk lid

Here are two skills summaries in essay form:

As a member of the soccer team, I've learned how to work well with others. There are many different personalities on the team, and I've learned to use teamwork to accomplish a goal. Without teamwork, it is hard to be successful. I have to listen to my coaches and teammates and follow directions. Along with listening and understanding, I have learned to voice my opinions. Being a member of this team has helped me learn to respect others' ideas. With these skills, I am hoping to become a captain of the team next year.

I am competent in allocating my time, following schedules, and budgeting my money. I am involved in my church, my community, a few clubs, and various sports. I also maintain a part-time job. I have learned from experience to make and to keep schedules and to prioritize when conflict occurs. My various activities have also taught me the importance of budgeting my paycheck to cover the costs of maintenance for my car, club dues, sports equipment, and savings for college. Through my participation in these activities, I've become good at being punctual and managing my time and expenses. Following schedules, budgeting money, and allocating time are just a few of my competencies.

Credentials

This part of your career portfolio contains all formal documents that you have received both in school and from outside sources. You should keep the original documents in your portfolio and make copies to leave with employers.

Put original documents in your portfolio, and make copies for employers.

Your credentials include the following:

- ✔ High school diploma

- ✔ Certificates of completion

- ✔ Certificates of recognition (honor roll, attendance, extracurricular activities, and so on)

- ✔ Awards of distinction

- ✔ All other honors received

Optional Items

Here is a list of other items that you can include in your career portfolio:

- ✔ **School profile:** Describes the educational environment of your school, such as accreditation, grading system, honors courses, and so on.

- ✔ **List of accomplishments:** Describes extracurricular and job activities that are not directly related to your career goal and are not included on your resume.

✔ **Letters of recommendation:** Written by teachers, coaches, advisors, past employers, and anyone else who thinks highly of you.

✔ **Examples of your work:** Depending on your situation, you can include samples of your art, photographs of a project, audiotapes, videotapes, images of Web pages you developed, and other media that can provide examples of your work.

✔ **Sports vita if applying for a sports scholarship:** Can include statistics, newspaper articles, and photos that provide examples of your involvement in sports.

✔ **Documentation of community service:** Can include photos, timesheets, or letters from supervisors reporting on your community services.

How to Package Your Portfolio

Your career portfolio is a personal reflection of you. The more effort you put into it, the more impressive the final outcome will be. Your portfolio can be the first impression of the following:

✔ Who you are

✔ What you are

✔ What you want to become

Your portfolio can be as simple or as elaborate as you want it to be. There are many different ways to make a portfolio; only your creativity, time, and budget limit you. For example, you may want to use a three-ring binder or a two-pocket folder, or your high school may provide you with a leather-bound portfolio with your school emblem on it. Or you may want to create your own Web site that presents printable documents and examples of your Web or other skills.

Presenting your portfolio will require you to review the contents and be ready to point out the things that will most impress an employer. Be sure to zero in on your strengths. Finally, be prepared with extra copies of your resume and other materials that an employer may want to keep.

Your portfolio can be as simple or as elaborate as you want it to be.

ACTIVITY

Plan Your Career Portfolio

List the items to include in your portfolio. Your teacher will guide you if your school has additional or different requirements than those listed in this chapter.

CAREER PORTFOLIO WORKSHEET

_____

_____

_____

_____

_____

_____

_____

_____

_____

_____

_____

_____

_____

_____

_____

_____

_____

_____

_____

ACTIVITY

Create a Digital Portfolio

A digital portfolio, also known as an electronic portfolio, contains all the information from your career portfolio in an electronic format. This material is then copied onto a CD-ROM or published on a Web site. With a digital portfolio, you can present your skills to a greater number of people than would see your paper career portfolio. Also, colleges and employers often prefer to receive applications and resumes in an electronic format. By completing this activity, you will also develop the information, systems, and technology SCANS skills that you need to be a successful employee.

DIGITAL PORTFOLIO PLAN WORKSHEET

Digital portfolios can contain a wide variety of media, such as digital pictures, video, PowerPoint presentations, and word processing documents. Your digital portfolio should include your best work and anything that demonstrates your strongest work-related skills. Look over the list you created on the Career Portfolio Worksheet. Are there any other items that you want to include in your digital portfolio? List them here.

_____

_____

_____

_____

_____

_____

Many items in your career portfolio may already be in a digital format. For example, you created your resume using word processing software. (If you used a school or library computer, make sure you have an electronic copy of the file on a disc so that you can include it in your digital portfolio.) You might only have paper copies of other items, such as artwork or letters of recommendation. To create electronic versions of your career portfolio materials, you need to use many different tools. For example, you would need a scanner to create an electronic copy of a paper high school transcript. List the types of equipment and software you would need to complete your digital portfolio:

_____

_____

_____

_____

_____

Portfolios, especially digital ones, need to be organized clearly so that employers or college admissions people can easily find information. On a Web site, the opening page, or home page, contains links to major topics. These topics then link to related documents, photos, or videos. This list of links works like a table of contents in a book.

Use a separate sheet of paper to draw a chart showing how you plan to organize information on your digital portfolio Web site.

> "You can't build a reputation on what you're going to do."
>
> *Henry Ford*

Chapter 13

Organize Your Job Search

Very few job seekers have had formal training on career planning or job seeking. The few who do have a big advantage over those who don't. Now it's time to put the information from this workbook into action. This chapter will help organize your schedule to make your job search a success.

The Objective of Your Job Search: To Get an Offer for a Good Job

To get a job offer, you must get interviews. To get interviews, you must organize your job search. Before you learn how to organize your job search, let's discuss some important details.

The average job seeker gets about five interviews per month—fewer than two interviews per week. Yet many job seekers using JIST techniques find it easy to get two interviews per day. To do this, you have to redefine what an interview is. Here is our definition:

> *An interview is face-to-face contact with anyone who has the authority to hire or supervise a person with your skills. The person may or may not have a job opening at the time of the interview.*

With this definition, it is much easier to get interviews. You can now interview with all sorts of potential employers, not just with those who have job openings. Remember that you can get interviews by doing the following:

✔ Use the yellow pages and make about an hour of phone calls. Use the telephone contact script discussed in Chapter 7.

✔ Drop in on potential employers and ask for an unscheduled interview. Job seekers get interviews this way—not always, of course, but often enough.

✔ Reach prospective employers with the help of technology—Web sites, e-mail, and fax. (Of course, there's always the U.S. mail, too.)

Getting two interviews per day equals 10 per week and more than 40 per month. That's 800 percent more interviews than the average job seeker gets. Who do you think will get a job offer more quickly?

Knowing and doing are two different things. Your job at this time is to pull together what you have learned and make a plan of action.

Use a Job Search Calendar

To be an effective job seeker, you need a job search calendar. The average job seeker spends about five hours per week actually looking for work. The average person is also unemployed an average of three or more months. People who follow JIST's advice spend much more time on their job search each week. They also get jobs in less than half the average time—often much less than half. So your job search calendar should include the following:

Calendar

April 2012 ◀▶

Mo	Tu	We	Th	Fr	Sa	Su
26	27	28	29	30	31	1
2	3	4	5	6	7	8
9	10	11	12	13	14	15
16	17	18	19	20	21	22
23	24	25	26	27	28	29
30	1	2	3	4	5	6

Calendar
Meetings
Group Calendars
Trash

✔ The number of hours per week you plan to look for work

✔ The days and hours you will look

✔ The job search activities you will do during these times

This chapter has three job search calendar activities. The first worksheet helps you make basic decisions about your weekly schedule. The second worksheet shows you how to create your own schedule for one day of the week. The last worksheet helps you put those two parts together to make a job search calendar for one week.

TIP

When completing your calendar, assume that you are out of school, unemployed, and looking for a full-time job. In a real sense, you are scheduling your job as if it were a job itself. This calendar will become the model for your actual job search.

ACTIVITY

Part One: Basic Decisions About Your Job Search

Complete the worksheet that follows. Keep these questions and points in mind:

✔ **How many hours per week?** After you are out of school, how many hours per week do you plan to look for a job? We suggest at least 25 hours if you are unemployed and looking for a full-time job. If 25 hours seems like too many, select a number you feel sure you can keep. Write the number on the bottom of the worksheet.

✔ **What days will you look?** Mondays through Fridays are the best days to look for most jobs, but weekends are good for some jobs. Put a check mark in the Yes column of the worksheet for each day you plan to spend looking for a job.

✔ **How many hours each day?** You should decide how many hours to spend on your job search each day. It is usually best to put in at least three or four hours each day you look for work. Write the number of hours on the worksheet.

✔ **What times will you begin and end on each of these days?** The best times to contact most employers are 8 a.m. to 5 p.m. Write these hours on the worksheet.

BASIC DECISIONS ABOUT YOUR JOB SEARCH SCHEDULE

Day of Week	✔ Yes	No	Time Start/Stop	Hours per Day
Sunday			to	
Monday			to	
Tuesday			to	
Wednesday			to	
Thursday			to	
Friday			to	
Saturday			to	
			Total Hours per Week_____	

ACTIVITY

Part Two: Your Daily Job Search Plan

You now need to decide how to spend your time each day. This is important, because most job seekers find it hard to stay productive. You already know which job search methods are most effective, and you should plan to spend more of your time using these. The sample daily schedule that follows has been effective for those who have used it. It will give you ideas for your own schedule.

Sample Daily Job Search Schedule

Time	Activity
7:00 to 8:00 a.m.	Get up, shower, dress, eat breakfast, get ready to go to work.
8:00 to 8:15 a.m.	Organize my workspace. Review schedule for interviews and promised follow-ups. Update schedule as needed.
8:15 to 9:00 a.m.	Review old leads for follow-up. Develop 20 new leads (want ads, yellow pages, networking lists, Internet exploration, and so on).
9:00 to 10:00 a.m.	Make phone calls. Set up interviews.
10:00 to 10:15 a.m.	Take a break.
10:15 to 11:00 a.m.	Make more calls.
11:00 a.m. to noon	Make follow-up calls as needed.
Noon to 1:00 p.m.	Lunch break.
1:00 to 3:00 p.m.	Go on interviews. Make cold contacts in the field. Research potential employers at the library, on the Internet, and at the local bureau of employment services.

Use the following worksheet to create your own schedule for a typical day. Use blank sheets of paper as needed.

JOB SEARCH PLAN FOR A TYPICAL DAY

Time		Plan of Action
Start	**End**	

Time		Plan of Action
Start	**End**	

Time		Plan of Action
Start	**End**	

Time		Plan of Action
Start	**End**	

Time		Plan of Action
Start	**End**	

Time		Plan of Action
Start	**End**	

Time		Plan of Action
Start	**End**	

ACTIVITY

Part Three: Your Job Search Calendar

Use the information that you developed in this chapter to create a calendar for the typical week of someone who is using the JIST method for looking for work (much more than five hours per week). Look at the following sample, and then make your own on the blank worksheet. Keep in mind that your goal is to get interviews. Try to reach that goal in steps. Strive for the following:

✔ Three to four interviews during the first week.

✔ At least one interview per day during the second week.

✔ Two interviews per day during the third and additional weeks. Keep going until success comes your way and you get the job you want.

DAYS OF THE WEEK							
TIME	**Sunday**	**Monday**	**Tuesday**	**Wednesday**	**Thursday**	**Friday**	**Saturday**
8:00		Organize day					Day off
9:00	Read want ads	Gather old and new leads					
10:00		Make phone contacts					
11:00		Follow up Get 2 interviews					
noon	Lunch	Write/ send follow-up correspondence					
1:00	Explore Internet	Plan afternoon Lunch					
2:00			Leave for interview	Drop off resume at printer	Appt. with Lisa at Whitman Co.	Afternoon off!	
3:00		Work on resume	Interview at Fischer Brothers		Pick up resume		
4:00			Make final revisions on resume		Drop by state employment office		
5:00	Dinner						
6:00	Read job search books						

WEEKLY JOB SEARCH CALENDAR WORKSHEET

DAYS OF THE WEEK

Time	Sunday	Monday	Tuesday	Wednesday	Thursday	Friday	Saturday
8:00							
9:00							
10:00							
11:00							
noon							
1:00							
2:00							
3:00							
4:00							
5:00							
6:00							

If You Use an Electronic Scheduler

You can easily adapt the ideas presented in this chapter to work on any electronic planning system. After you work out your daily and weekly job search schedule, transfer it to your electronic scheduler and use its reminder alarm and other features to organize your follow-up and other tasks.

Find a job you like and you add five days to every week.

H. Jackson Brown, Jr.

ACTIVITY

Get the Job You Want

Keep the following questions and pointers in mind for getting the job you want. The blank spaces after each section are for your thoughts and notes.

GETTING THE JOB YOU REALLY WANT WORKSHEET

1. **Know the job you want.**

   ✔ Do not ask for just "any job you have."

   ✔ Why do you want the job?

   ✔ What skills do you have to do the job well?

   ✔ What is the salary range for this type of job?

   ✔ What other jobs require similar skills?

   _____

   _____

   _____

   _____

2. **Know what the employer is looking for.**

   ✔ Are you a good, hard worker?

   ✔ Can the employer depend on you to be on time, have good attendance, and do the job?

   ✔ Do you appear to really want this job and say so?

   ✔ If you don't have the best experience, can you overcome this?

   ✔ Will you stay with the organization?

   ✔ Will you become sick or injured?

✔ Do your good points outweigh your weaknesses?

_____

_____

_____

_____

3. **Know where to look.**

✔ Small businesses hire about two-thirds of all people. Keep them in mind.

✔ Spend more time with the most effective job search methods: networking and direct contacts with employers.

✔ Network with friends, relatives, and acquaintances for job leads and for names of other people to contact.

✔ Use the yellow pages to find and contact large and small employers.

✔ Explore company information on the Internet.

✔ Use traditional job lead sources: want ads, state employment services, and others.

_____

_____

_____

_____

4. **Know how to look.**

✔ Always apply alone.

✔ Organize and make a job search schedule.

✔ Send thank-you notes.

✔ Stay in touch with employers and anyone who might help you get job leads.

(continued)

(continued)

✔ Use the phone to save time in setting up interviews and in following up.

✔ Get lots of interviews. Even if no openings exist now, you may be considered for future ones.

✔ Do well in interviews and follow up. If you want the job, say so.

_____

_____

_____

_____

_____

5. **Think.**

✔ Even if you haven't had a job before, you have abilities and skills that some employer needs.

✔ Communicate your background and skills on the phone; in person; through your portfolio; and on your JIST Card, resume, and applications.

✔ Be prepared, and know how to answer problem questions in interviews.

✔ Learn from your failures in addition to your successes.

✔ Find out the reasons you were turned down and overcome them in the next interview.

✔ If you can't get one type of job, look for another.

✔ Don't be afraid of asking questions. If you don't know something, ask.

_____

_____

_____

_____

6. **Keep trying.**

   ✔ You must apply for work to get it.

   ✔ There are openings every day for most skills—but the openings may be hard to find.

   ✔ Make your job search into a job itself.

   ✔ Spend at least 25 hours per week looking for work.

   ✔ Set your goal of getting two interviews per day.

   ✔ Don't give up. You are a good person, and you will make it.

   _____

   _____

   _____

   _____

   _____

   _____

7. **A few more tips.**

   ✔ Think before accepting the first job offer you receive.

   ✔ Don't quit looking just because you have a job offer.

   ✔ The more offers you get, the better chance you have at a good job rather than just "a job."

   _____

   _____

   _____

   _____

   _____

   _____

The JIST Formula for Getting a Good Job

Here is the simple formula for getting a good job:

Yellow Pages + Cold Contacts + Networking with Your Warm Contacts = Job Leads

Job Leads = Interviews

Interviews = Job Offers

Job Offers = A Job!

Chapter 14

Tips to Survive and Get Ahead on a New Job

Getting a good job is important, but keeping one is, too. If you do well, you may be able to move up to a better job—or use what you learn to get a better job. During the years you work, you will have many different jobs. Most people change careers at least three times and hold 8 to 10 jobs in their working lives. Each new job will bring about changes in your life, and each will present chances to learn and problems to overcome. This chapter will help you get off to a successful start.

Success on the Job

As you begin a new job, you may feel a bit unsure because you don't know what to expect. Will you get along with the other people who work there? Are you dressed right? Will you be able to handle the new responsibilities?

The information in this chapter will help you feel more confident and become a successful employee.

Most people give up just when they're about to achieve success. They quit on the one yard line. They give up at the last minute of the game one foot from a winning touchdown.

H. Ross Perot

Get Off to a Good Start—Meet Employer Expectations

You were hired because the employer felt you had the skills and abilities needed to get the job done. You now will be expected to become a productive employee. This is your chance to prove that you really do meet all three major employer expectations: appearance, dependability, and skills.

Expectation #1: Appearance

Here are some things to consider when beginning a new job:

- ✔ **Self-image:** Show confidence in the way you present yourself.

- ✔ **Dress:** Be neat and clean in your appearance and grooming. Dress appropriately for the type of job you are starting.

- ✔ **Personality:** Be natural and friendly, and show respect to your coworkers and supervisors. Don't forget to smile.

- ✔ **Communications:** Use good verbal skills when you talk to others. Show your interest by asking questions and being positive.

- ✔ **Behavior:** Be cooperative with others, and work hard at adjusting to the work routine expected of you. Find someone to help you learn the basics of the job.

Expectation #2: Dependability

One way to prove that you are worthy of your new job is to show that you are dependable. All employers expect you to be reliable. Make the following a part of your daily job habits:

- ✔ **Be at work on time:** Arrive a few minutes early. Allow yourself enough travel time by considering the traffic situation and the route you will take.

- ✔ **Follow the expected work schedule:** Take only the time allowed for breaks and lunch. Be sure to arrive back at your workstation on the scheduled time or a few minutes early.

Allow yourself enough travel time to arrive a few minutes early.

✔ **Know what duties you should be performing:** Be sure that you complete what is expected of you. Ask your supervisor to explain any special procedures or rules to you. Ask for and read at home any personnel and procedural materials related to your job.

✔ **Don't miss work:** A minor illness (like a cold) is not a good reason for missing work, and neither is a personal problem (such as childcare). If you miss more than three days per year for these reasons, it may be too much.

✔ **Call if you will be absent or late:** If you will be more than a few minutes late or absent for any reason, call in at the beginning of the workday. Talk directly to your supervisor and explain the situation. Do not leave a message. Sometimes, you may be able to call the day before if you think there could be a problem.

Expectation #3: Skills

Your performance on the job will show the employer whether he made the right choice in hiring you. How well will you measure up?

✔ **Show that you have the skills:** Then apply them daily.

✔ **Strive to improve your skills:** Develop new ways to do a better job.

Look for ways to be efficient on the job.

✔ **Seek ways to learn new skills:** Learn all you can from any job you have. Do the job as well as you are able. Look for ways to spend your time more efficiently.

✔ **Accept responsibility:** Take responsibility for your job and your performance.

✔ **Know company policies:** Read personnel and procedure manuals.

✔ **Work quickly but carefully:** Perform at a steady and quick pace. Find a pace that you can keep up all day without making errors.

✔ **Be willing to take on additional responsibilities:** Try your best to do something extra when you are asked. Volunteer for tasks that allow you to learn something new.

TIP Don't wait until a formal review to find out how you are doing on your job. Ask your supervisor for feedback on ways you can improve your job performance.

Other Expectations

✔ **Stay away from problem employees:** Some people tend to be negative about their jobs. Others do things against the rules, waste time, or in other ways are not good workers. These people may be fun to be with, but spending time with them will affect your performance. Your coworkers and supervisors may begin to see you as a problem. Be friendly, but do not socialize with people like this any more than is necessary.

✔ **Keep personal activities and problems at home:** You are paid to get a job done. Making personal phone calls, paying bills, coming back late from lunch, or talking to other staff about what you did last weekend are not what you are being paid to do. Although socializing for a few minutes on the job is acceptable, you can easily overdo it.

TIP Limit your personal activities and discussions to breaks, lunch times, and hours outside of work.

✔ **Manage children and other family members:** Although children or other family members may be the most important part of your life, they are not your employer's concern. Make sure that childcare arrangements are in place prior to accepting a job. If your children are in school, arrange childcare so that you do not miss work when they are ill. Strongly discourage personal phone calls except in emergencies. When interviewing for a job, tell employers that you will be a dependable worker and that childcare has been arranged. Assure them that you needn't miss work for this reason.

Why People Get Fired: The Employer's Point of View

Everyone wants to be accepted and successful on a new job. Surviving on the job may mean that you have to change the way you act and some of your attitudes.

One way to survive on a job is to make sure that you avoid the things that get people fired. Here are the top 10 reasons employers give for firing people. The top 3 are listed first.

✔ **Dishonesty:** This is one of the top reasons employers give for firing some-one. More employers are now screening new applicants to eliminate people who have been dishonest with previous employers. Employers don't want to pay someone who steals from them or can't be trusted.

✔ **Slow work:** This is a major reason for job failure. You can see why: Unproductive employees cost more than they earn. A slow worker is expensive compared to another worker who gets the same job done in less time.

✔ **Refusal to follow orders or get along with supervisor:** In a battle with a supervisor, you will almost always lose.

✔ **Unreliability; too many days absent or late:** When an employee is absent, it disrupts the work of others. These people may have to neglect their work to make up for the absent worker. Being late sets a bad example for others and often disrupts others' work.

✔ **Inability to get along with other workers:** Many workers consider this problem one of the top reasons they don't like their jobs. Although few employers list it among the top reasons for firing someone, it is often a factor. You don't have to like all the people you work with, but you need to be able to get along with them.

✔ **Poor attire or grooming:** The way you look is significant. This is particularly true in office jobs and in jobs where you deal with customers. Poor dress and grooming affect how the employer feels about you. This can be one of many things that a terminated employee did not do well.

✔ **Too many mistakes:** Someone who makes mistakes can be costly to an employer. Perhaps another employee has to spend time correcting errors. A customer may become unhappy with the company's products or services as a result of sloppy work. That customer doesn't come back and tells others about the bad experience.

✔ **Accident-prone; refusal to follow safety rules:** Employers do not want to keep people who have accidents or who do not follow safety rules. Accidents can be costly to employers and dangerous to other employees.

✔ **Inability to do the work:** Few people get fired because they could not do the work. Employers tend to hire people they think can do the job and then give them time to learn it.

✔ **Abuse of alcohol or drugs:** Substance abuse is a major problem in some organizations. A person who abuses alcohol or drugs often gets fired for being unreliable or for some other reason. The employer may not even know the cause of the problem.

There are many reasons why an employer might fire a person. Almost any reason can be enough if it is a serious problem. More often, however, people are fired for more than one reason. For example, they may be late to work too often and make too many mistakes.

TIP There are many reasons people lose their jobs. If this happens to you, learn from the experience and look for a new job that does not present the same problems.

Tips on Handling Work Conflicts

Two of the top 10 reasons why people get fired have to do with the ability to get along with other people at work, either supervisors or coworkers. One important part of being able to get along with other people is being able to handle conflicts and disagreements in a fair and peaceful way without causing additional problems. The following tips will help you handle disagreements at work:

✔ **Talk directly to the person involved:** Unnecessarily involving supervisors and other workers in a problem just makes the problem worse. Don't contribute to office gossip by discussing the problem with others who are not involved.

✔ **Control your emotions:** Make sure you are calm before you try to confront someone about a problem. Yelling or crying will not help you find a solution and may make others lose respect for you.

✔ **Stay positive:** Don't just complain about problems—offer solutions. Find points where you agree with the other person and work from there to find a compromise.

> "The way a team plays as a whole determines its success."
>
> *Babe Ruth*

ACTIVITY

Get Off to a Good Start on Your Job

You need to start a new job with a good attitude and thorough preparation.

GOOD START WORKSHEET

List the issues and problems that may get in your way when starting a new job. Also think of tasks you need to do before starting the job, such as arranging for transportation. Then list a solution to each issue or the steps you need to take to complete the task. Example: *Issue*—I tend to oversleep. *Solution*—Get to bed earlier and use two alarm clocks.

Issue, Problem, or Task	Solution or Steps to Be Taken

Get Ahead and Move Up on the Job

If you want to advance on your job, you have to do more than the minimum. Here are some extra things you can do to help you get ahead:

1. **Dress and groom for a promotion.**

   * If you want to get ahead in an organization, dress and groom as if you worked at the level you hope to reach next. This is not always possible, but at the very least, be clean and well groomed.

   * Wear clothes that fit well and look good on you. Copy the clothing styles of others who are successful in the organization. Even when your coworkers see you away from work, present the image you want for yourself at work.

2. **Be early and stay late.**

   * Get to work a few minutes early. Use this time to list what you plan to get done that day. At the end of the day, leave a few minutes after quitting time.

   * Be willing to stay late to meet an important deadline. If you stay late, let the boss know. Stay late only when you have an important deadline to meet, unless you are asked.

3. **Be enthusiastic.**

   * Go out of your way to find ways to enjoy your job. Tell others what you like about it, particularly those you work with. Emphasize those parts of your job that you like to do and do well. Share this enthusiasm even in conversations with your friends.

   * Make a particular effort to tell your supervisor what you like about your job. This will help you focus on the parts of your job you are most likely to want to do more of. It will also help others notice that you do them well.

4. **Ask for more responsibility.**

   * As soon as you begin a new job, look for ways to learn new things.

   * Volunteer to help out in ways you feel will make you more valuable to the organization.

   * Let the boss know you want to move up.

   * Ask for advice about what you can do to be more valuable to the organization.

5. **Ask how you can earn more money.**

   * In your first week on the job, ask your supervisor to see you for about 30 minutes of private time. When you have his or her attention, say that you want to be more valuable to the organization. Ask what you can do to get a raise as soon as possible. One suggestion is to request special assignments to help develop your skills.

   * Before you leave the meeting, ask for a specific future date to go over your progress and what you have to do to get the raise. Ask the boss to give you feedback on your progress from time to time.

6. **Ask for training.**

   * Get as much training as possible! If the training sounds interesting or useful but is outside of your job responsibilities, request it anyway.

   * Define the type of training you need to do your job better, and look for it outside the organization. Explain to your supervisor how the training will help the organization. Ask for help in finding the best training source.

7. **Take on difficult projects.**

   * You won't get much attention unless you do more than what is expected of you. Look for projects that you think you can do well and that would benefit the organization in some clear way.

   * Don't promise too much, and keep a low profile while you do the work. If no one expects too much, it is easier to be seen as successful even if your results are not as good as you had hoped.

8. **Get measurable results.**

   * Keep records of what you do. Compare them to past performance or the average performance of others in similar situations. If your results look good, send a report to your supervisor. For example, if the number of orders went up 40 percent over the same month last year with no increase in staff, that's a big accomplishment.

   * Look for ways to present what you do in numbers, such as dollars saved, percentage of sales increased, number of persons served, number of units processed, and size of budget.

A Word About Character

The kind of worker you are has a lot to do with the kind of person you are. Chapter 3 discussed the importance of self-management skills, also known as character traits. These traits may not have gotten you the job, but they help you keep a job and move ahead. The following traits have been identified as important to workplace success:

✔ **Honesty:** Of course, you shouldn't steal from your employer or cheat customers—after all, dishonesty is one of the top reasons people are fired. But honesty also means admitting when you have made a mistake.

✔ **Responsibility:** Employers need to know that you will show up on time and do the work you were hired to do.

✔ **Positive attitude:** Workers who are enthusiastic about their work and are willing to learn new tasks are more likely to be successful.

Look for opportunities both on the job and in your personal life where you can demonstrate these traits and build on them. Working to improve your character will not only help you advance in your career, but it also will help you grow as a person.

When You Leave a Job

Many people leave their jobs because they don't like the people they work with. People may also be unsatisfied with their jobs for reasons related to money, stress, advancement, and other factors. If you are thinking about leaving your job, here are some points to consider first:

✔ **Don't just quit:** If the job is not working out for you, ask for a job change within the organization before you give up. If you are unhappy with your job and decide to leave, do not talk about it to anyone who works with you until you have found another job. Some people lose their jobs when the boss finds out they are unhappy or planning to leave.

✔ **Look for another job before quitting:** If possible, begin your job search while you are still employed. You can update your resume, set up interviews before and after work, or take vacation time to look.

✔ **Notify your employer:** After you decide to leave, give 30 days' notice if at all possible. Two weeks' notice is the minimum you should give.

✔ **Give a positive but honest reason for leaving:** Examples might be that you've found a job with more growth opportunity or that you've decided to go back to school. A positive but honest reason is better than complaints, a burst of anger, or not giving any reason. You never know when you'll encounter your boss again.

✔ **Give a written notice:** Give a formal letter of resignation to your supervisor when you tell him or her, in person, that you are leaving. Stress the positive experiences you have had and the good feelings you have about the people you worked with. See the sample resignation letter on the next page.

When quitting, leave your job with a positive attitude.

✔ **Complete all your job responsibilities:** This is especially important if you are working on an individual project or a team effort. Be prepared to train a new person in your job.

✔ **Leave your present position with a positive attitude:** Say goodbye to people whom you have worked with most closely. Don't hold grudges or bad-mouth anyone.

✔ **Ask for a letter of reference:** Make this request to your supervisor before you leave. If you did well, the letter will be positive, and it is much easier to get it now. If there were problems, at least you will know what your current boss will say about you to future employers.

Resignation Letter Example

Here is a sample letter you can use as a guide. Be sure to include the following:

✔ Your final date of employment

✔ Your reason for leaving

✔ Your personal thanks for the skills you have learned, for the supervisor's support, and for your coworkers' help

47 Mill Run Drive
Orange, California 99999
February 20, 20XX

Ms. Roberta Gordon
Johnson Corporation
2222 Industrial Road
Los Angeles, California 99999

Dear Ms. Gordon:

Please accept this letter as notice of my resignation, effective March 15, 20XX.

Last day of work

I have accepted a position as quality control assistant with the Harper Corporation and am to report to work on March 30, 20XX.

Reason for quitting

Thank you for your interest in me, and I want you to know that I will miss everyone I have worked with here.

A personal thank-you

Sincerely,

June Hernandez

June Hernandez

Create Your Own Job

You know just what you want to do, and you are certain that people will pay for the service you can provide or the product you can create. The problem is that after researching on the Internet and using other job search methods, you haven't found an employer that offers the kind of job you're looking for. Maybe you could work for yourself instead. According to the U.S. Bureau of Labor Statistics, about 7 percent of the workforce is self-employed. Have you ever considered starting your own business? The Are You an Entrepreneur activity on the next page can help you decide.

ACTIVITY

Are You an Entrepreneur?

Entrepreneurs are people who turn their ideas into successful businesses. Take this quiz to find out if you share characteristics with successful entrepreneurs. Write Yes in the blank if you agree with the statement, and No if you disagree with the statement.

DISCOVERING YOUR ENTREPRENEURAL POTENTIAL

____ 1. I am a good salesperson.

____ 2. I prefer solving problems on my own instead of solving them with a group.

____ 3. I can usually find more than one answer to a problem.

____ 4. I am energetic and rarely get sick.

____ 5. I can accept uncertainty without worrying about it.

____ 6. I would rather work on a project that I am passionate about than relax.

____ 7. I dislike people telling me how to do things because I want to do things my own way.

____ 8. I am confident in my abilities.

____ 9. I see failure as a learning experience instead of a reason to give up.

____ 10. I am competitive.

Add the number of Yes answers you have and write the total here: ____

If you answered Yes to seven or more statements, you have many of the characteristics of an entrepreneur. Even if you answered No to most of the statements, you may develop these characteristics as you gain education and job experience and discover work that you are passionate about.

ACTIVITY

Your Own Business

Businesses sell either products or services. Entrepreneurs often start businesses that relate to jobs they have had or hobbies they enjoy. Think about what you like to do and how you could turn that into a business, and then answer the following questions. You will probably have to do some research first.

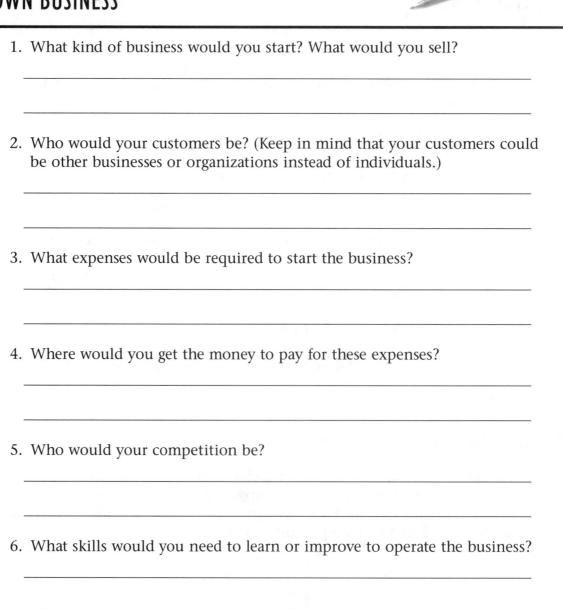

STARTING YOUR OWN BUSINESS

1. What kind of business would you start? What would you sell?

   _____

   _____

2. Who would your customers be? (Keep in mind that your customers could be other businesses or organizations instead of individuals.)

   _____

   _____

3. What expenses would be required to start the business?

   _____

   _____

4. Where would you get the money to pay for these expenses?

   _____

   _____

5. Who would your competition be?

   _____

   _____

6. What skills would you need to learn or improve to operate the business?

   _____

   _____

The End—and a Beginning

You now know much more about looking for work than most people your age. Although this book ends here, so much more is to come for you. We offer a few closing thoughts:

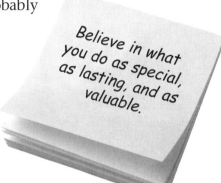

Believe in what you do as special, as lasting, and as valuable.

✔ **Don't be afraid to try things:** You will probably have many jobs during the years ahead—some good, some not so good. Each one will teach you something and help you in some way for the future.

✔ **Decide to do something worthwhile:** Whether it is raising a family or saving old-growth forests, believe in what you do as special, as lasting, and as valuable.

✔ **Work well:** All work is worth doing, so put your energy into it and do it as well as you are able.

✔ **Enjoy life:** It's sort of the same as having fun, but it lasts longer and means more.

✔ **Send thank-you notes:** Many people will help you throughout your life in large and small ways. Let them know you appreciate it. The more you give, the more you seem to get in return.

We wish you good fortune in your job search and in your life!

APPENDIX

Get Career Information and Figure Out a Job Objective

This book assumes that you already have a good idea of the kind of job you want. If you do, this appendix can give you additional information on learning about the many types of jobs in your career area.

If you're not sure what you want to do after high school, that's okay, too. Most young people try a variety of jobs before they settle into one job or career area. You may also need to earn some money while going to school or feel that you just want to goof off awhile before getting serious about working.

Whatever your situation, it is to your advantage to know how to find out about the many careers available and to concentrate on the ones that seem most interesting. The U.S. Department of Labor provides job descriptions for more than 1,100 jobs. That is far more than you can hope to learn about during this course.

There are many ways to find out more about jobs. This appendix lists some of the most useful ways to explore careers and use career resources.

Counseling Resources

Career counseling: Your school is often a good source of information and advice. Make sure you know what services are available and that you use them.

Testing resources: You can take a variety of vocational tests to learn more about your interests and abilities. Following are brief comments on the most popular types:

✔ **Interest tests** allow you to compare the things that interest you to what people do in various careers. Most of these tests then suggest careers, career clusters, or additional education. Your school may use paper-and-pencil tests or computerized tests.

✔ **Ability tests** are quite different. They compare what you know and what you can do to the skills of people who already work in various fields. A carpenter, for example, needs to be good with his hands and be able to use various measuring tools. If you do well on the test in manual dexterity and basic math, the test might suggest that carpentry is one field you could do well in. You might not like working with your hands, but the test doesn't consider this. Ability tests may or may not be used in your school. Like interest tests, they can be in the form of paper and pencil or be computerized.

✔ **Other tests** may be available from your school counselor. All these tests can be helpful in some way. But tests are not magic. They can't give you final answers and are often incomplete. You should trust your own sense of what is right for you and do that. Tests can be wrong, and many people are doing—and enjoying—jobs that the tests said they wouldn't be good at. Trust yourself above all else.

Printed Resources

Career materials at the library: Career-related books and journals are available at most libraries. Check your school and public library for information on careers that interest you. Also ask at the library about journals and magazines that people who work in these fields read. These publications are excellent sources for current, field-specific information.

Occupational Outlook Handbook (OOH): We consider this one of the most helpful sources of career information. Most school counseling offices and libraries have this book. Published by the U.S. Department of Labor, it lists more than 270 of the most popular jobs in the country. Two-thirds of all people work in these jobs. The *OOH* is updated every two years, so try to get the most current edition.

The jobs are organized into clusters of related occupations. This makes it easy to find jobs that seem interesting and to consider ones that you may not have thought about before. The description for each job includes information on working conditions, future openings, related jobs, pay scales, training required, and other details. Because it is updated every two years, the information is current, and the descriptions are well done.

The jobs covered in the *OOH* are listed at the end of this section. Look up the jobs you are interested in and read about them in the *OOH*. Schools can obtain copies of the *OOH* from JIST.

New Guide for Occupational Exploration: Based on the 16 U.S. Department of Education interest areas, the *New Guide for Occupational Exploration* provides a helpful method of exploring careers, guiding you in using your interests, education, previous experience, skills, and other factors to find your career. JIST publishes the *New Guide for Occupational Exploration.*

Other Resources

People: Much of what you know about various jobs has probably come from other people. Ask your parents and others what they do and do not like about their jobs. Then compare this to your own likes and dislikes. When you identify a job that really interests you, find someone who does that work and ask him or her to tell you more about it.

The Internet: The Internet offers an enormous amount of information on careers and education. Ask your teacher or a librarian for good sites for this information.

Entry-level and volunteer jobs: Many young people can get jobs in fields that interest them for careers. If you want to work in the medical field, for example, try to get a job in a hospital or other medical facility. Hospitals also use volunteers in various roles. You may be able to turn unpaid experience into a paying job.

Working your way up: You may have to start at the bottom and work your way up. Young people can often take an entry-level job and use it to show that they can work hard and be trusted.

For example, if you have never managed a business, few employers would hire you to run one. But you might be able to get a job as a stock clerk and then learn as much as possible about the business. Let the employer know that you want more responsibility. Be willing to take on new tasks. Even if you can't move up in that job, you can use what you learn to get a better job in the future.

Occupational Outlook Handbook Occupations Listing

Use this listing to find jobs that seem interesting to you. Then look up the description for the jobs that interest you most in the Occupational Outlook Handbook. *The brief descriptions there include useful information on working conditions, skills needed, education and training required, earnings, related jobs, and more.*

Management, Business, and Financial Operations

Management
Administrative services managers
Advertising, marketing, promotions, public relations, and sales managers
Computer and information systems managers
Construction managers
Education administrators
Engineering and natural sciences managers
Farmers, ranchers, and agricultural managers
Financial managers
Food service managers
Funeral directors
Human resources, training, and labor relations managers and specialists
Industrial production managers
Lodging managers
Medical and health services managers
Property, real estate, and community association managers
Purchasing managers, buyers, and purchasing agents
Top executives

Business and Financial Operations
Accountants and auditors
Budget analysts
Claims adjusters, appraisers, examiners, and investigators
Cost estimators
Financial analysts and personal financial advisors
Insurance underwriters
Loan counselors and officers
Management analysts
Tax examiners, collectors, and revenue agents

Professional

Computer and Mathematical
Actuaries
Computer programmers
Computer software engineers
Computer support specialists and systems administrators
Computer systems analysts, database administrators, and computer scientists
Mathematicians
Operations research analysts
Statisticians

Architects, Surveyors, and Cartographers
Architects, except landscape and naval
Landscape architects
Surveyors, cartographers, photogrammetrists, and surveying technicians

Engineers
Aerospace engineers
Agricultural engineers
Biomedical engineers
Chemical engineers
Civil engineers
Computer hardware engineers
Electrical and electronics engineers, except computer
Environmental engineers
Industrial engineers, including health and safety
Materials engineers
Mechanical engineers
Mining and geological engineers, including mining safety engineers
Nuclear engineers
Petroleum engineers

Drafters and Engineering Technicians
Drafters
Engineering technicians

Life Scientists
Agricultural and food scientists
Biological scientists
Conservation scientists and foresters
Medical scientists

Physical Scientists
Atmospheric scientists
Chemists and materials scientists
Environmental scientists and geoscientists
Physicists and astronomers

Social Scientists
Economists
Market and survey researchers
Psychologists
Social scientists, other
Urban and regional planners

Science Technicians

Community and Social Services
Clergy, including Protestant ministers, rabbis, and Roman Catholic priests
Counselors

Probation officers and correctional treatment specialists

Social and human service assistants

Social workers

Legal

Court reporters

Judges, magistrates, and other judicial workers

Lawyers

Paralegals and legal assistants

Education, Training, Library, and Museum

Archivists, curators, and museum technicians

Instructional coordinators

Librarians

Library technicians

Teacher assistants

Teachers—adult literacy and remedial and self-enrichment education

Teachers—postsecondary

Teachers—preschool, kindergarten, elementary, middle, and secondary

Teachers—special education

Art and Design

Artists and related workers

Designers

Entertainers, Performers, and Sports

Actors, producers, and directors

Athletes, coaches, umpires, and related workers

Dancers and choreographers

Musicians, singers, and related workers

Media and Communications

Announcers

Broadcast and sound engineering technicians and radio operators

Interpreters and translators

News analysts, reporters, and correspondents

Photographers

Public relations specialists

Television, video, and motion picture camera operators and editors

Writers and editors

Health Diagnosing and Treating Practitioners

Audiologists

Chiropractors

Dentists

Dietitians and nutritionists

Occupational therapists

Optometrists

Pharmacists

Physical therapists

Physician assistants

Physicians and surgeons

Podiatrists

Recreational therapists

Registered nurses

Respiratory therapists

Speech-language pathologists

Veterinarians

Health Technologists and Technicians

Cardiovascular technologists and technicians

Clinical laboratory technologists and technicians

Dental hygienists

Diagnostic medical sonographers

Emergency medical technicians and paramedics

Licensed practical and licensed vocational nurses

Medical records and health information technicians

Nuclear medicine technologists

Occupational health and safety specialists and technicians

Opticians, dispensing

Pharmacy technicians

Radiologic technologists and technicians

Surgical technologists

Veterinary technologists and technicians

Service

Healthcare Support

Dental assistants

Medical assistants

Medical transcriptionists

Nursing, psychiatric, and home health aides

Occupational therapist assistants and aides

Pharmacy aides

Physical therapist assistants and aides

Protective Service

Correctional officers

Firefighting occupations

Police and detectives

Private detectives and investigators

Security guards and gaming surveillance officers

Food Preparation and Serving-Related Occupations

Chefs, cooks, and food preparation workers

Food and beverage serving and related workers

Building and Grounds Cleaning and Maintenance

Building cleaning workers

Grounds maintenance workers

Pest control workers

Personal Care and Service

Animal care and service workers

Barbers, cosmetologists, and other personal appearance workers

Childcare workers

Flight attendants

Gaming services occupations

Personal and home care aides

Recreation and fitness workers

Sales

Cashiers

Counter and rental clerks

Demonstrators, product promoters, and models

Insurance sales agents

Real estate brokers and sales agents

Retail salespersons

Sales engineers

Sales representatives, wholesale and manufacturing

Sales worker supervisors

Securities, commodities, and financial services sales agents

Travel agents

Office and Administrative Support

Communications equipment operators

Computer operators

Customer service representatives

Data entry and information processing workers

Desktop publishers

Financial clerks, including bill and account collectors; billing and posting clerks and machine operators; bookkeeping, accounting, and auditing clerks; gaming cage workers; payroll and timekeeping clerks; procurement clerks; tellers

Information and record clerks, including brokerage clerks; credit authorizers, checkers, and clerks;

file clerks; hotel, motel, and resort desk clerks; human resources assistants, except payroll and time-keeping; interviewers; library assistants, clerical; order clerks; receptionists and information clerks; reservation and transportation ticket agents and travel clerks

Material-recording, -scheduling, -dispatching, and -distributing workers, including cargo and freight agents; couriers and messengers; dispatchers; meter readers, utilities; production, planning, and expediting clerks; shipping, receiving, and traffic clerks; stock clerks and order fillers; weighers, measurers, checkers, and samplers, record-keeping

Office and administrative support worker supervisors and managers

Office clerks, general

Postal service workers

Secretaries and administrative assistants

Farming, Fishing, and Forestry

Agricultural workers

Fishers and fishing vessel operators

Forest, conservation, and logging workers

Construction Trades

Boilermakers

Brickmasons, blockmasons, and stonemasons

Carpenters

Carpet, floor, and tile installers and finishers

Cement masons, concrete finishers, segmental pavers, and terrazzo workers

Construction and building inspectors

Construction equipment operators

Construction laborers

Drywall installers, ceiling tile installers, and tapers

Electricians

Elevator installers and repairers

Glaziers

Hazardous materials removal workers

Insulation workers

Painters and paperhangers

Pipelayers, plumbers, pipefitters, and steamfitters

Plasterers and stucco masons

Roofers

Sheet metal workers

Structural and reinforcing iron and metal workers

Installation, Maintenance, and Repair

Electronic Equipment

Computer, automated teller, and office machine repairers

Electrical and electronics installers and repairers

Electronic home entertainment equipment installers and repairers

Radio and telecommunications equipment installers and repairers

Vehicle and Mobile Equipment

Aircraft and avionics equipment mechanics and service technicians

Automotive body and related repairers

Automotive service technicians and mechanics

Diesel service technicians and mechanics

Heavy vehicle and mobile equipment service technicians and mechanics

Small engine mechanics

Other Installation, Maintenance, and Repair

Coin, vending, and amusement machine servicers and repairers

Heating, air-conditioning, and refrigeration mechanics and installers

Home appliance repairers

Industrial machinery installation, repair, and maintenance workers, except millwrights

Line installers and repairers

Maintenance and repair workers, general

Millwrights

Precision instrument and equipment repairers

Production

Assemblers and Fabricators

Food-Processing Occupations

Metal Workers and Plastic Workers

Computer-control programmers and operators

Machine setters, operators, and tenders—metal and plastic

Machinists

Tool and die makers

Welding, soldering, and brazing workers

Printing

Bookbinders and bindery workers

Prepress technicians and workers

Printing machine operators

Textile, Apparel, and Furnishings

Woodworkers

Plant and System Operators

Power plant operators, distributors, and dispatchers

Stationary engineers and boiler operators

Water and liquid waste treatment plant and system operators

Other Production

Dental laboratory technicians

Inspectors, testers, sorters, samplers, and weighers

Jewelers and precious stone and metal workers

Ophthalmic laboratory technicians

Painting and coating workers, except construction and maintenance

Photographic process workers and processing machine operators

Semiconductor processors

Transportation and Material Moving

Air Transportation

Air traffic controllers

Aircraft pilots and flight engineers

Motor Vehicle Operators

Bus drivers

Taxi drivers and chauffeurs

Truck drivers and driver/sales workers

Rail Transportation Occupations

Water Transportation Occupations

Material Moving Occupations

Job Opportunities in the Armed Forces

Index